COLLINS
PHRASE BOOKS

SPANISH

Collins Phrase Books

FRENCH
GERMAN
ITALIAN
PORTUGUESE
SPANISH
SCANDINAVIAN
RUSSIAN
GREEK
YUGOSLAV
DUTCH
LATIN AMERICAN SPANISH

85

COLLINS
PHRASE BOOKS

SPANISH

Compiled by
DONALD S. GIFFORD

COLLINS
LONDON AND GLASGOW

First Published 1965
Latest Reprint 1978

Cover photographs for cased
edition by courtesy of
J. Allan Cash Ltd. (top)
Colour Library International Ltd. (bottom)

ISBN Cased 0 00 433904 5
ISBN Limp 0 00 433924 X
© William Collins Sons & Co. 1965

Printed in Great Britain
Collins Clear-Type Press

CONTENTS

CONTENTS

ÍNDICE DE MATERIAS

INTRODUCTION

This little book is more than a collection of useful phrases. It also answers many of the questions which a traveller in the Spanish-speaking countries will wish to ask about food, travel, customs and so on.

Of course, it is not possible to give precise details about all these things, because timetables, rates of exchange, passport and customs regulations change. Up-to-date information may be obtained from travel agencies. Labour exchanges also supply information about passports, and banks about currency rates and regulations. A table is provided on page 140 in which the current rate of exchange should be entered.

Trains

There are four types of train in Spain: the *Talgo* (Irun–Madrid) and the *Taf* (from principal coast towns, e.g. Santander, Seville–Madrid) are fast luxury trains; the *expreso* is first and second class only; the *rápido* and *correo* have all three classes and are slow, though recommended for local colour and the "common touch." Other trains have long halts for meals although Spaniards usually take food with them, e.g. cold chops, omelettes, etc. Sleeping-car travel, when available, is good and about the same price as in England. Second class travel is comfortable; some third class compartments have wooden seats. Travellers are advised to book well in advance through an Agency or R.E.N.F.E., since, in the summer especially, there is a great shortage of seats in coast-bound trains. The booking office at the station is open for about one hour before the train leaves, and closes five minutes before the departure of the train.

Local Information

This may be obtained in any city from the *Oficinas de Información de la Dirección General del Turismo*.

Meals

In Spain breakfast consists of coffee and rolls. Lunch and dinner are the main meals and these meals are usually served at about 2 p.m. and 9 p.m. respectively. Afternoon tea is not provided in hotels unless specially ordered.

All milk is boiled, hence tea without milk is preferable where

available. *Merienda* is either a picnic tea or an early meal for childre
where specially requested. Except at breakfast, *coffee* means blac
coffee.

The café is very popular in Spain, and provides a constant meetir
place for friends or for discussion. Spaniards are very hospitabl
talkative and helpful to foreigners.

Tipping

Where a percentage service charge is made, as in restaurants and hotel
an extra tip is optional. One tips porters about 8 pesetas per ite
of luggage, a nightwatchman (*sereno*) about 4 pesetas and taxi drive
and waiters anything from 10% to 15%.

Amusements

Good cinemas are to be found in all Spanish towns; usually or
theatre specialises in programmes of folk music and dancing. Lig
musical entertainment is known as *revista*, but the *zarzuela*, a live
musical comedy of Madrid life, is unique. Other musical shows ma
have *flamenco* singing and dancing.

Bull-fighting is mainly a summer entertainment, and although
bull-fight usually takes place once a week in most large towns, the goc
fights are generally only to be seen during *fiesta* times. The sma
bull-fights provide all that is unpleasant in the spectacle withou
affording the visitor any display of skill or artistry.

Motoring (*see also section* MOTORING)

Full information regarding motoring abroad may be obtained fro
the Automobile Association or the Royal Automobile Club, wh
also issue the requisite documents. The A.A. or R.A.C. are able 1
supply current information about the amount of petrol and c
available and the approximate prices.

General Advice (*see section* POLICE, PASSPORTS AND FORMS abou

the compulsory registration of foreigners)
Visitors are advised to observe as far as possible the general custom
of the country in matters relating to dress. Shorts, either for men c
women, are not acceptable, except as beach apparel, and all bathin
costumes must conform to certain standards. Failure to observe th
regulations may result in a fine being imposed by a beach guarc
though restrictions are becoming less severe. Women should see tha
their heads, arms and legs are covered on entering a church and me
should not enter in shorts.

Note on Using a Dictionary

The symbols *ch* and *ll* are placed separately in the Spanish alphab
after c and l respectively, hence *chico* will not be found under c, nc
llave under l.

SCHEME OF PRONUNCIATION

The following scheme is similar to that of *Collins Spanish Gem Dictionary*. It sacrifices complete accuracy to simplicity, but being based on English pronunciation it should be easily understood and used by those whose native speech is English even when they have no knowledge of phonetics.   A more energetic delivery is normal in Spanish than is often the case in English. The vowels are represented by only one letter and, unlike those of English, maintain the same sound throughout their length, (cf. Spanish c*o*sa, and English h*o*me). Every letter is pronounced except *h,* and *u* in *que* and *qui.*

Vowels

	Comment	English spelling used	Example
a	as in p*a*ssport, never as in p*a*rent	a	p*a*dre
e	as in Scottish English s*ay,*	ay	c*e*na
	also as in p*e*n	e	*e*l
i	always as in mach*i*ne, never as in s*i*de	ee	n*i*ño
o	as in *oh*! also as in *o*n (the difference is made naturally)	o	p*o*ngo
u	as in m*oo*n	oo	l*u*mbre
u+e	silent		Mig*u*el
u+i	silent		g*uí*a
u+a	as in *wa*n	w	g*ua*rdia
y	as in gentr*y*	ee	m*uy*

Consonants

	Comments	English spelling used	Example
b	almost as in English initially,	b	*b*anco
	but generally more like v	"	ha*b*a
c+a	as in *c*at	k	*c*alle
c+o	as in *c*omb	"	*c*ola
c+u	as in *c*ool, but also as in q*u*ack	"	*c*ura
		kw	*cu*ando
c+e	as in *th*ane	th	*c*ena
c+i	as in *th*ree	"	*c*ita
c+h	as in *ch*in, never as in ma*ch*ine	ch	*ch*ica

d	initially and after n, as in _dog_	d	_donde_
	between vowels and finally, as in _then_	dh	_tostada*_
f	as in English	f	_feo_
g+a	as in _gasp_	g	_gato_
g+o	as in _go_	„	_gordo_
g+u	as in _gun_ (see also u)	„	_gula_
g+e	as in Scottish lo_ch_	h	_gente_
g+i	as in Scottish lo_ch_	„	_gitano_
h	always silent		_hombre_
j	as in Scottish lo_ch_	h	_caja_
k	as in English	k	_kilómetro_
l	as in English	l	_listo_
ll	as in mi_lli_on	ly	_calle_
m	as in English	m	_madre_
n	as in English	n	_niño_
ñ	as in _onion_	ny	_niño_
p	as in English	p	_padre_
q+u	as in _k_ing, (never as in _qu_estion)	k	_quisiera_
r	always pronounced	r	_pero_
rr	strongly trilled	rr	_perro_
s	always hissed, (never as in the_s_e)	s	_casa_
t	as in English	t	_toalla_
v	as in English with lips almost together	v	_vino_
w	like English v	v	_wagon_
x	mostly as in English	x	_exacto_
y	as in _you_	y	_yo_
z	as in _thi_n	th	_cerveza_

* does not apply to the second-last _d_ of a word ending in —_da_
e.g. ciu_d_ad, which is hard.

The above remarks apply to Castilian or Standard Spanish (_castellano_). The following differences are to be found in Latin Americ_a_ and Southern Spain.

ll	as in _you_, and also	_calle_
	as in inva_si_on	„
c+e	as in _ce_ntre	_cena_
c+i	as in _ci_ty	_ciudad_
z	as in _s_ay	_cerveza_
d	silent when final and between vowels	_tostada_
		ciudad
s	sometimes like _h_	_tostada_

Stress or Accentuation It is possible to pronounce each letter correctly and still not be understood if the wrong syllable is stressed he rules are:—

) Words ending in a VOWEL, N or S stress the *second-last* yllable: m*a*no, h*o*mbre. par*a*guas, ex*a*men.

) Words ending in a CONSONANT (other than N or S) stress the *last* yllable: am*o*r, far*o*l, ciud*a*d.

A departure from these rules calls for a written accent: pap*á*, til, raz*ó*n, ej*é*rcito.

Diphthongs:—*a*, *o*, *e* are strong vowels and *u*, *i* are weak. Strong + eak (or weak + strong): stress the strong: b*o*ina, su*e*lo. Strong + rong counts as two syllables, stress the second: ma*e*stro. Weak + eak, stress the second: ru*i*do.

A departure from these rules again calls for a written accent: ba*ú*l, e o*í*do.

GRAMMATICAL NOTES

hese do not aim at completeness but are a framework into which the aveller (whom we visualise as wanting to speak the language rather an read novels in it) may fit the words and phrases of this book. ccordingly two narrative tenses (the Past Historic and the Imperfect) ave been omitted, and also the 2nd person singular. One or two ementary notions of gender, particularly, are worth acquiring as el mujer" or "yo hablar", for instance, sound ludicrous to Spanish ars.

Nouns

ender: Male and female beings fall into the appropriate gender, but ings are also masculine (words ending in -o) or feminine (words ding in -a).

Words ending in *e* or a consonant may fall into one or the other:
 hombre, el dinero, el papel   are masc.
 xceptions: la mano, la radio
 chica, la carta, la llave   are fem.
 xceptions: el día, el tranvía, el idioma, el mapa, el programa, el oblema, el telegrama, el sistema, etc.

ural: The plural is formed by adding -s or -es:
    puerta → puertas; hombre → hombres

Definite Article (the)

	Singular	*Plural*
Masc.	el libro	los libros
Fem.	la carta	las cartas

El instead of *las* is used with nouns beginning with stressed *a* or *h* (without changing the gender):
la acción, las aguas, but el agua
la hacienda, las hachas, but el hacha.

Indefinite Article (a, an)

	Singular	Plural
Masc.	un libro	(unos) libros
Fem.	una carta	(unas) cartas

The plural may be used to indicate *some*.
The indefinite article is omitted before a few adjectives including
otra vez=another time; tal cosa=such a thing; cien libras=a hundred
pounds.

Demonstratives (this, etc.)

	Singular	Plural
Masc.	este libro=this book	estos libros=these books
	ese aquel } „=that book	esos aquellos } „=those books
	Singular	Plural
Fem.	esta carta =this letter	estas cartas =these letters
	esa aquella } „ =that letter	esas aquellas } „ =those letters

The demonstrative pronoun is no different to the ear: este libro
y aquél=this book and that one.

Adjectives

Agreement: adjectives ending in -o, agree as follows:

	Singular	Plural
Masc.	un pueblo bonito=a pretty town	pueblos bonitos
Fem.	una carta larga=a long letter	cartas largas

Adjectives ending in -e or a consonant merely add -s or -es for the
plural. But those of nationality in -és, have four forms:

	Singular	Plural
Masc.	inglés (English)	ingleses
Fem.	inglesa	inglesas

Position: it will be noticed that adjectives generally follow their noun.
They may precede it, and some in this case shorten in the masculine
singular: un buen hotel=a good hotel; el primer día=on the first
day; el mal hombre=the bad man; ningún dinero=no money; algún
amigo=some friend.

Comparison:
bonito =pretty   más bonito =prettier   el más bonito=prettiest
bueno   =good   mejor   =better   el mejor   =best

malo =bad   peor   =worse   el peor   =worst
malísimo=very bad.
tanto dinero como usted=as much money as you.

Interrogatives
¿Qué hombre? =What man?   cf. ¡Qué hombre! =What a man!
¿Cuál sombrero?=Which hat?   ¿Cuántos   How many
   artículos?   =   articles?

Numbers: do not agree up to one hundred:
cuatro mujeres=four women. But: doscientas pesetas=200 pesetas
   note: cien pesetas   =100 pesetas

Possessives: agree with the thing possessed and not with the possessor.
The most useful to know are:
mi=my; nuestro=our; su=his, her, their, your.
They are used as follows:

	Singular		*Plural*
Masc.	*Fem.*	*Masc.*	*Fem.*
mi libro	mi carta	mis libros	mis cartas
nuestro libro	nuestra carta	nuestros libros	nuestras cartas
su libro	su carta	sus libros	sus cartas

Pronouns

	Subject		*Object*
Singular	yo=I	*Singular*	me=me
	*usted=you		le (masc.) la (fem.)=you
	él=he, it		lo=him, it
	ella=she, it		la=her, it
Plural	nosotros=we	*Plural*	nos=us
	*ustedes=you		les (masc.) las (fem.)=you
	ellos } =they		los } them
	ellas }		las }

*Of the subject pronouns, only these (often written Vd. and Vds.)
are used if emphasis or clarity is desired.

Position: object pronouns are normally placed before the verb:
Ustedes *nos* conocen=You know *us*. But not:
1) in the positive imperative: ¡Démelo!   =Give me it!
2) with an infinitive: Voy a verle   =I am going to see him.
3) with a present participle: Estoy lavándome   =I am washing.

Possessive pronouns: mine=el mío, etc. with four forms agreeing with
the nouns referred to.

ours=el nuestro, etc. with four forms agreeing with the nouns referred to.
his, hers, theirs, yours=el suyo, etc. with four forms agreeing with the nouns referred to.
e.g.: nuestro país y el suyo=our country and yours.

Interrogative Pronouns
¿Quién?=Who?   ¿Qué?=What?   ¿Cómo?=How?
¿Cuándo?=When?   ¿Cuánto?=How much? ¿Dónde?=Where?

Relative pronoun: que will generally suit:
el hombre que veo=the man whom I see.

Questions, Negatives and Indefinites
1) One may ask a question by reversing normal word-order and placing Subject after Verb: ¿Nada Vd.?=Do you swim?
   One may do so by raising the voice: ¿Vd. nada?
2) No entiendo   =I do not understand
   No he entendido   =I did not understand
3) ¿Desea Vd. algo?   =Do you want something?
   No deseo nada   =I do not want anything.

Verbs
A knowledge of only four forms in each tense will normally suffice. The present, perfect (called here the past) and future are listed as being the most useful to the traveller. The Imperative is given separately and many examples of its use occur in the body of the book. Notice that usted and ustedes are really third person.

Verbs like HABLAR=TO SPEAK

Present Tense	Past Tense	Future Tense
hablo I speak	he hablado	hablaré
habla you, he, she speak(s)	ha hablado	hablará
hablamos we speak	hemos hablado	hablaremos
hablan they, you speak	han hablado	hablarán

Verbs like APRENDER=TO LEARN

aprendo	he aprendido	aprenderé
aprende	ha aprendido	aprenderá
aprendemos	hemos aprendido	aprenderemos
aprenden	han aprendido	aprenderán

Verbs like **VIVIR**=**TO LIVE**

vivo	he vivido	viviré
vive	ha vivido	vivirá
vivimos	hemos vivido	viviremos
viven	han vivido	vivirán

Verbs like **ENTENDER** (i →ie)=**TO UNDERSTAND**

entiendo	he entendido	entenderé
entiende	ha entendido	entenderá
entendemos	hemos entendido	entenderemos
entienden	han entendido	entenderán

Verbs like **CONTAR** (u →ue)=**TO COUNT, EXPECT**

cuento	he contado	contaré
cuenta	ha contado	contará
contamos	hemos contado	contaremos
cuentan	han contado	contarán

Verbs like **PEDIR** (e →i)=**TO ASK FOR, ORDER**

pido	he pedido	pediré
pide	ha pedido	pedirá
pedimos	hemos pedido	pediremos
piden	han pedido	pedirán

Reflexive verbs, like **LEVANTARSE**=**TO GET UP**

me levanto	me he levantado	me levantaré
se levanta	se ha levantado	se levantará
nos levantamos	nos hemos levantado	nos levantaremos
se levantan	se han levantado	se levantarán

Irregular verbs   **SER**=**TO BE**

soy	he sido	seré
es	ha sido	será
somos	hemos sido	seremos
son	han sido	serán

used 1) with nouns: es estudiante=he is a student
2) with so-called permanent adjectives like: bueno=good; malo=bad; hermoso=beautiful; feo=ugly; pequeño=small; grande =big; rico=rich; pobre=poor; joven=young; viejo=old.

ESTAR=TO BE

estoy	he estado	estaré
está	ha estado	estará
estamos	hemos estado	estaremos
están	han estado	estarán

used 1) to indicate position: está aquí=he is here
2) with so-called temporary adjectives such as: bien (or bueno) =well; malo (or enfermo)=ill; cansado=tired; ocupado=busy; contento=pleased; muerto=dead.

TENER=TO HAVE, POSSESS

tengo	he tenido	tendré
tiene	ha tenido	tendrá
tenemos	hemos tenido	tendremos
tienen	han tenido	tendrán

IR=TO GO

voy	he ido	iré
va	ha ido	irá
vamos	hemos ido	iremos
van	han ido	irán

VENIR=TO COME

vengo	he venido	vendré
viene	ha venido	vendrá
venimos	hemos venido	vendremos
vienen	han venido	vendrán

DECIR=TO SAY, TELL

digo	he dicho	diré
dice	ha dicho	dirá
decimos	hemos dicho	diremos
dicen	han dicho	dirán

HACER=TO DO, MAKE

hago	he hecho	haré
hace	ha hecho	hará
hacemos	hemos hecho	haremos
hacen	han hecho	harán

DAR=TO GIVE

doy	he dado	daré
da	ha dado	dará
damos	hemos dado	daremos
dan	han dado	darán

VER=TO SEE

veo	he visto	veré
ve	ha visto	verá
vemos	hemos visto	veremos
ven	han visto	verán

The Imperative: is formed
1) regularly, by using the non-characteristic vowel: ¡com*a*!=Eat!
¡Levánt*e*se vd!=Get up!
2) irregularly, rather like the first person singular present tense:
¡Salga!=leave! ¡Dígame!=Tell me!

Adverbs
These are regularly formed by adding -mente to the adjective:
distinta-mente=distinctly; general-mente=generally.
Note: bien=well; mal=badly; rápido=quickly.

COMMON WORDS AND PHRASES

VOCABULARY

how?, ¿cómo? (kó-mo)
how much?, ¿cuánto(a)? (kwán-to/a)
how many?, ¿cuántos(as)? (kwán-tos/as)
when?, ¿cuándo? (kwán-do)
where?, ¿dónde? (dón-day)
why?, ¿por qué? (por káy)

above, por encima de (por en-thēē-ma day)
according to, según (say-gōōn)
after, después de* (des-poo-áys day)
against, contra (kón-tra)
almost, casi (ká-see)
also, también (tam-bee-én)
always, siempre (see-ém-pray)
among, entre (én-tray)
and, y (ee)
around, alrededor de* (al-ray-dháy-dhór day)
at, a (a), en (en)
at once, en seguida (en say-gēē-dha)
backwards, atrás (a-trás)
because, porque (pór-kay)
before, antes de* (án-tays day)
behind, detrás de* (day-trás day)
below, debajo de* (day-bá-ho day)
beside, al lado de* (al lá-dho day)
besides, además (a-dhay-más)
between, entre (én-tray)
during, durante (doo-rán-tay)
early, temprano (tem-prá-no)
elsewhere, en otra parte (en ó-tra pár-tay)
everywhere, en todas partes (en tó-dhas pár-tays)
except, excepto (es-thép-to)
far, lejos (láy-hos)
for, para (pára), por (por)
forwards, adelante (a-dhay-lán-tay)
here, aquí (a-kēē)
in: into, en (en)
in order to, para (pá-ra)
inside, dentro de* (dén-tro day)
less, menos (máy-nos)
little, a, un poco (oon pó-ko)
many, muchos(as) (mōō-chos/as)

23

more, más (mas)
much(a) (mōō-cho/a)
near, cerca de* (tháyr-ka day)
on, en (en), sobre (só-bray)
only, sólo (só-lo), solamente (so-la-mén-tay)
opposite, en frente (en frén-tay)
outside, fuera de* (foo-áy-ra day)
over, por encima de* (por en-thēē-ma day)
over there, por allí (por al-yēē)
quickly, rápido (rá-pee-dho)
scarcely, a penas (a páy-nas)
since (time), desde (dés-day)
since (because), puesto que (poo-áys-to kay)
slowly, despacio (days-pá-thee-o)
so (+adj.), tan (tan)
so (manner), así (a-sēē)
so much/many, tanto(a) (os) (as) (tán-to)
sometimes, algunas veces (al-gōō-nas váy-thays)
soon, pronto (prón-to)
then, entonces (en-tón-thays)
there, allí (al-yēē)
through, por (por)
too (too much), demasiado (day-mas-ee-á-dho)
towards, hacia (á-thee-a)
under, debajo de* (day-bá-ho day)
until, hasta (ás-ta)
upstairs, arriba (a-rēē-ba)
very, muy (mwee)
well, bien (bee-én)
without, sin (seen)
yet, todavía (to-dha-vēē-a)
*de is dropped in adverbial use

POLITE EXPRESSIONS

When addressing strangers to ask the way, etc., one should begin
Perdóneme (per-dó-ne-me); a gentleman is addressed politely as *Señor*
(sen-yór); a lady as *Señora*, (sen-yó-ra) and if unmarried as *Señorit*
(sen-yo-rēē-ta). *Don* and *Doña* (dón-ya) are forms of address, used only with
christian names and for rather more elderly people. Telephone operators
are addressed as *Señorita*; waitresses as *Camarera* (ka-ma-ré-ra) and waiter
as *Camerero* (ka-ma-ré-ro) or *Mozo* (mó-tho).
   Note.—In addressing children, Spaniards use the familiar *tu* form of
the verb. Small children use this form when speaking to most adults
older children learn to distinguish, hence will address the visitor as *usted*.

Good morning sir.	Buenos días señor.
	bwáy-nos dēē-as sayn-yór
Good afternoon (evening) madam.	Buenas tardes señora.
	bwáy-nas tár-days sayn-yó-ra
Goodnight miss.	Buenas noches señorita.
	bwáy-nas nó-chays sayn-yo-rēē-ta
Hello. Good-bye.	¡Ola! Adiós.
	ó-la a-dhee-ós
Good-bye (in the meantime)	Hasta luego.
	á-sta loo-áy-go
Till we meet again.	Hasta la vista.
	á-sta la vēēs-ta
Yes. No.	Sí. No.
	see no
Please.	Por favor; haga el favor.
	por fa-vór; á-ga el fa-vór
Thank you.	Gracias.
	grá-thee-as
Thank you very much.	Muchas gracias.
	mōō-chas grá-thee-as
This is Mr. . . .	Le presento al Señor. . . .
	lay pray-sén-to al sen-yór . . .
Glad to meet you. How do you do.	Mucho gusto señor.
	mōō-cho gōōs-to sen-yór
How are you?	¿Cómo está usted?
	kó-mo es-tá oos-táydh
Very well—and you?	Muy bien—¿y usted?
	mwee bee-én ee oos-táydh
With pleasure.	Con mucho gusto.
	kon mōō-cho gōōs-to
I'm sorry. Excuse me.	Perdone.
	per-dó-nay
Pardon?	¿Perdone?
	per-dó-nay

I'm very sorry.	Lo siento mucho.
	lo see-én-to mōō-cho
May I?	¿Con su permiso?
	kon su per-mēē-so
Please sit down.	Siéntese por favor.
	see-én-tay-say por favór
You are very kind.	Usted es muy amable.
	oos-táydh es mwee a-má-blay
Don't mention it.	No hay de qué. De nada.
	no á-ee day kay. day ná-dha
May I help you?	¿Puedo ayudarle?
	poo-áy-dho a-yoo-dhár-lay
Did you want something?	¿Deseaba usted algo?
	day-say-á-ba oos-táydh ál-go
Help yourself.	Sírvase usted mismo.
	sēēr-va-say oos-táydh mēē-smo
Don't bother.	No se moleste.
	no say mo-lés-tay
I'm sorry to disturb you.	Siento molestarle.
	see-én-to mo-les-tár-lay
It's no trouble.	No es ninguna molestia.
	no es neen-gōō-na mo-lés-tee-a
Your good health!	¡Salud!
	sa-lōōdh
Congratulations!	¡Felicitaciones!
	fay-lee-thee-ta-thee-ó-nays
I am glad to see you.	Me alegro de verle.
	may a-láy-gro day vér-lay
I am much obliged to you.	Le estoy muy agradecido.
	lay es-tóy mwee a-gra-dhay-thēē-dho
Thank you for your hospitality.	Le agradecemos su hospitalidad.
	lay a-gra-dhay-tháy-mos su os-pee-tah-lee-dádh
We enjoyed ourselves very much.	Nos divertimos mucho.
	nos dee-ver-tēē-mos mōō-cho

As you please.   Como quiera usted.
                              kó-mo kee-áy-ra oos-táydh

I'd like to.   Yo quisiera.
                              yo kee-see-áy-ra

MISCELLANEOUS EXPRESSIONS

What is your name?   ¿Cómo se llama usted?
                              kó-mo say lyá-ma oos-táydh

My name is . . .   Me llamo . . .
                              may lyá-mo . . .

I am British (American).   Soy inglés (inglesa) (norte-
                                     americano/a).
           soy een-gláys (een-gláy-sa) (nor-tay-a-may-ree-ká-no/a)

Do you understand (speak)   ¿Entiende (habla) usted
  Spanish?   español?
           en-tee-én-day (á-bla) oos-táydh es-pan-yól

I speak it a little.   Lo hablo un poco.
                              lo á-blo oon pó-ko

Look out!   ¡Cuidado!
                              kwee-dá-dho

I don't know.   No sé.
                              no say

On the contrary.   Al contrario.
                              al kon-trá-ree-o

That's right.   ¡Eso es!
                              áy-so es

Listen. Look.   Escuche. Mire.
                              es-kōō-chay. mēē-ray

Very well.   Muy bien.
                              mwee bee-én

That's all.   Es todo.
                              es tó-dho

Whose turn is it?	¿A quién toca?
	a kee-én tó-ka

Go. Come.   Vaya. Venga.
                       vá-ya. vén-ga

I must go.   Tengo que marcharme.
                 tén-go kay mar-chár-may

It is getting late.   Se hace tarde.
                 say á-thay tár-day

Are you ready?   ¿Está usted listo(a)?
            es-tá oos-táydh lēēs-to(a)

As soon as possible.   Cuanto antes.
                 kwán-to án-tays

At the latest.   A más tardar.
                 a mas tar-dár

Don't forget.   No olvide.
                 no ol-vēē-dhay

Don't be late.   No llegue tarde.
                 no lyáy-gay tár-day

I'm glad.   Me alegro.
                 may a-láy-gro

I believe so.   Creo que sí.
                 kráy-o kay see

I'm not surprised.   No me extraña.
                 no may es-trán-ya

Isn't that so?   ¿No es verdad?
                 no es ver-dádh

Isn't it? Aren't you?   ¿Verdad?
(cf. French *n'est-ce pas?*)
                 ver-dádh

I'm hungry (thirsty, sleepy,   Tengo hambre (sed, sueño,
right, hot, cold, frightened).   razón, calor, frío, miedo).
   tén-go ám-bray (sed, swáyn-yo, ra-thón, ka-lór. frēē-o, mee-áy-dho)

Note: Other adjectives are used with *ser* or *estar*; *see* GRAMMATICAL
NOTES pp. 19-20.

You are mistaken.   Se equivoca.
                                     say ay-kee-vó-ka

On the left. On the right.   A la izquierda. A la derecha.
                          a la eeth-kee-áyr-da. a la day-ráy-cha

Straight on.   Todo derecho.
                                     tó-dho day-ráy-cho

Turn back.   Vuelva atrás.
                                     voo-áyl-va a-trás

Have you a light?   ¿Tiene usted lumbre?
                          tee-áy-nay oos-táydh lõõm-bray

Let's go for a walk.   Vamos a dar un paseo.
                          vá-mos a dar oon pa-sáy-o

DIFFICULTIES

I don't understand you.   No entiendo.
                                     no en-tee-én-do

I don't understand Spanish.   No entiendo el español.
                                     no en-tee-én-do el es-pan-yól

Do you understand English?   ¿Entiende usted el inglés?
                          en-tee-én-day oos-táydh el een-gláys

Is there anyone who speaks   ¿Hay alguien que hable
(understands) English?   (entienda) inglés?
                   á-ee ál-gee-en kay á-blay (en-tee-én-da) een-gláys

Please repeat it.   Repítalo por favor.
                          ray-pēē-ta-lo por fa-vór

Please speak more slowly.   Haga el favor de hablar más
                                          despacio.
                   á-ga el fa-vór day a-blár mas days-pá-thee-o

Please write it down.   Escríbalo por favor.
                          es-crēē-ba-lo por fa-vór

What is the matter?   ¿Qué hay?
                          kay á-ee

What do you want?	¿ Qué quiere usted ?
	kay kee-áy-ray oos-táydh
Wait, I am looking for the word (phrase) in this book.	Espere, busco la palabra (frase) en este libro.
	es-páy-ray, bōōs-ko la pa-lá-bra (frá-say) en és-tay lēē-bro
Will you read this?	¿ Sírvase leer esto ?
	sēēr-va-say lay-ér és-to
Where are you going?	¿ A dónde va usted ?
	a dón-day va oos-táydh
Come quickly!	¡ Venga rápido !
	vén-ga rá-pee-dho
My ... has been stolen.	Me han robado ...
	may an ro-bá-dho ...
That man is following me everywhere.	Ese hombre me sigue por todas partes.
	áy-say óm-bray may sēē-gay por tó-dhas pár-tays
I shall call a policeman.	Llamaré un policía.
	lya-ma-ráy oon po-lee-thēē-a
Fetch a policeman.	Mande buscar un guardia.
	mán-day boos-kár oon gwár-dee-a
I shall stay here.	Me quedaré aquí.
	may kay-dha-ráy a-kēē
Will you help me?	¿ Quiere usted ayudarme ?
	kee-áy-ray oos-táydh a-yoo-dhár-may
Help!	¡ Socorro !
	so-kó-ro
Fire!	¡ Hay fuego !
	á-eef oo-áy-go
Thief!	¡ Ladrón !
	la-drón
Who are you?	¿ Quién es usted ?
	kee-én es oos-táydh
What are you doing here?	¿ Qué hace usted aquí ?
	kay á-thay oos-táydh a-kēē
I don't know you.	No le conozco.
	no lay ko-nóth-ko

don't wish to speak to you.　　No quiero hablar con usted.
　　　　　　　no kee-áy-ro a-blár kon oos-táydh

eave me alone!　　　　　¡Déjeme!
　　　　　　　　day-hay-may

hat will do!　　　　　¡Basta!
　　　　　　　　bás-ta

have forgotten the word.　　He olvidado la palabra.
　　　　　ay ol-vee-dá-dho la pa-lá-bra

What does it mean?　　　¿Qué quiere decir?
　　kay kee-áy-ray day-thèèr

What have I done?　　　¿Qué he hecho?
　　　kay ay áy-cho

didn't know.　　　　No sabía.
　　　　no sa-bèè-a

lease explain to me.　　Explíqueme por favor.
　　es-plèè-kay-may por fa-vór

t wasn't me.　　　No fui yo.
　　　no fwee yo

t's not my fault.　　No es culpa mía.
　　no es kòòl-pa mèè-a

ll give you nothing.　　No le daré nada.
　　no lay da-ráy ná-dha

o away!　　　　¡Márchese!
　　　　már-chay-say

t has nothing to do with me.　No tiene nada que ver conmigo.
　no tee-áy-nay ná-dha kay ver kon-mèè-go

o whom does one apply?　¿A quién se dirige?
　　a kee-én say dee-rèè-hay

What must I do?　　　¿Qué debo hacer?
　　　kay dáy-bo a-thér

t is already paid for.　　Ya está pagado.
　　　ya es-tá pa-gá-dho

have paid enough.　　He pagado bastante.
　　ay pa-gá-dho bas-tán-tay

et me pass.　　　Déjeme pasar.
　　　day-hay-may pa-sár

Listen to me a moment. Escúcheme un momento.
es-kōō-chay-may oon mom-én-to

Stop him! ¡Deténgale!
day-tén-ga-lay

Call the police (a doctor). Llame la policía (un médico).
lyá-may la po-lee-thēē-a (oon máy-dhee-ko)

I am a foreigner. Soy extranjero.
soy es-tran-háy-ro

I am a stranger. Soy forastero.
soy fo-ras-táy-ro

I am (not) in a hurry. (No) tengo prisa.
(no) tén-go prēē-sa

How long must I wait? ¿Cuánto tengo que esperar?
kwán-to tén-go kay es-pay-rár

I am busy. Estoy ocupado.
es-tóy o-koo-pá-dho

I insist on it. Insisto en ello.
een-sēēs-to en él-yo

I promise you. Se lo prometo.
say lo pro-máy-to

I will give you my address. Le daré mis señas.
lay da-ráy mees sáyn-yas

Open the door! ¡Abra la puerta!
á-bra la poo-áyr-ta

Wait one moment. Espere un momento.
es-páy-ray oon mo-mén-to

What is the Spanish for that? ¿Como se dice eso en español?
kó-mo say déé-thay áy-so en es-pan-yól

Why not? ¿Por qué no?
por kay no

Where is the lavatory? ¿Dónde están los retretes?
dón-day es-tán los ray-tráy-tays

Where is the nearest police station? ¿Dónde está la comisaría mas cercana?
dón-day es-tá la ko-mee-sa-rēē-a mas ther-ká-na

Where is the British (American) consulate?

¿Dónde está el consulado británico (americano)?

dón-day es-tá el kon-soo-lá-dho bree-tá-nee-ko (a-may-ree-ká-no)

You do not understand.

Usted no entiende.

oos-táydh no en-tee-én-day

I am angry.

Estoy enfadado.

es-toy en-fa-dá-dho

I don't want it.

No lo quiero.

no lo kee-áy-ro

I've lost ...

He perdido ...

ay per-dée-dho

Can you tell me .. ?

¿Puede usted decirme ...?

poo-áy-dhay oos-táydh day-théēr-may

Tell him to wait.

Dígale que espere.

dée-ga-lay kay es-páy-ray

What do I owe you?

¿Qué le debo?

káy lay dáy-bo

POPULAR IDIOMS

It's terribly funny.

Me hace mucha gracia.

may á-thay mōō-cha grá-thee-a

You're pulling my leg.

Me toma el pelo.

may tó-ma el páy-lo

Really?

¿De veras?

day váy-ras

Never in your life.

Ni hablar.

nee a-blár

I say!

¡Oiga!

óy-ga

Let's get to the point.

Vamos al caso.

vá-mos al ká-so

You're joking of course.

Naturalmente lo dice en broma.

na-too-ral-mén-tay lo dée-thay en bró-ma

No kidding.	Sin mentira.
	seen men-tēē-ra
Likeable, nice (personality).	Simpático.
	seem-pá-tee-ko
Agreed. O.K.	Convenido.
	kon-vayn-ēē-dho
It is wonderful!	¡Es estupendo!
	es es-too-páyn-do
Encore!	¡Otra vez!
	ó-tra veth
How nice (of a person).	¡Qué simpático!
	kay seem-pá-tee-ko
How nice (of a thing).	¡Qué bonito!
	kay bo-nēē-to
Absolutely not!	¡En absoluto!
	en ab-so-lōō-to
Of course.	Desde luego.
	dés-day loo-áy-go
Of course not.	Claro que no.
	klá-ro kay no
It's not necessary.	No hace falta.
	no á-thay fál-ta
Good luck!	¡Mucha suerte!
	mōō-cha soo-áyr-tay
What bad luck!	¡Qué mala suerte!
	kay má-la soo-áyr-tay
So much the better (worse).	Tanto mejor (peor).
	tán-to may-hór (pay-ór)
Thank goodness!	¡Menos mal!
	máy-nos mal
What a nuisance!	¡Qué fastidio!
	kay fas-tēē-dhee-o
What a bore!	¡Qué aburrido!
	kay a-boo-rēē-dho
How awful!	¡Qué barbaridad!
	kay bar-ba-ree-dádh

How odd!	¡Qué raro! kay rá-ro
It doesn't matter.	No importa. no eem-pór-ta
What's on?	¿Qué echan? kay áy-chan
He is reliable.	Es muy formal. es mwee for-mál
He has the cheek of the devil.	Es una cara dura. es ōō-na ká-ra dōō-ra
My goodness!	¡Dios mío! dee-ós mēē-o
He is a rake.	Es un juerguista. es oon hoo-áyr-gēēs-ta
How stupid!	¡Qué disparate! kay dees-par-rá-tay
I couldn't care less.	No me da un bledo. no may da oon bláy-dho
Bless you! (*when someone has sneezed*)	¡Jesús! hay-sōōs
He is a tough.	Es un chulo. es oon chōō-lo
He is a pansy.	Es un maricón. es oon ma-ree-kón

PUBLIC NOTICES

Abierto=Open.
Aviso=Notice.
Caballeros=Gentlemen.
Caja=Cash Desk.
Carteles no=Stick no bills.
Cerrado=Closed.

Cuidado con la pintura=Wet Paint.
Empujad=Push.
Entrada=Way in.
Es peligroso asomarse=It is dangerous to lean out of the window.
Es propiedad=Private.
Libre=Vacant.
Ocupado=Engaged.
Oficina=Office.
Salida=Way out.
Salida de urgencia=Emergency Exit.
Se alquila=To let.
Señoras=Ladies.
Se prohibe . . .=It is forbidden to . . .
Se prohibe aparcar=No parking.
Se prohibe el canto=No singing.
Se prohibe escupir=No spitting.
Se prohibe fumar=No smoking.
Se prohibe la entrada=No entry.
Se prohibe pisar la hierba=Keep off the grass.
Se vende=For sale.
Tirad=Pull.

NATIONAL HOLIDAYS

National holidays.   Días festivos nacionales.
dēē-as fes-tēē-vos na-thee-on-a-lays

The list below may seem extensive, but many an unwary traveller has been dismayed to find banks and shops closed when he had most need of them. It includes political holidays established by the present régime which may not be permanent. On one's saint's day it is customary to treat one's friends. Children are often given presents at Epiphany (6th January, el día de Reyes) rather than Christmas.

New Year's Day.   El día del Año Nuevo.
el dēē-a del án-yo nwáy-vo

St. Joseph (19th March).	El San José. el san ho-sáy
Victory Day (1st April).	El día de la Victoria. el dēē-a day la veek-tó-ree-a
Holy Week.	Semana Santa. say-má-na sán-ta
Good Friday.	Viernes Santo. vee-ér-nays sánto
Easter.	Pascua. pás-kwa
Ascension Day (40 days after Easter).	La Ascensión. la as-then-sēē-on
Whitsun.	El Pentecostés. el pen-tay-kos-táys
Corpus Christi (Thurs. after Whitsun).	El Corpus. el kór-poos
Anniversary of Nationalist Rising (18th July).	El día del Alzamiento. el dēē-a del al-tha-mee-én-to
St. James (25th July).	El día de Santiago. el dēē-a day san-tee-á-go
Assumption (15th Aug.)	La Asunción. la a-soon-thee-ón
General Franco's birthday (1st Oct.)	El día del Caudillo. el dēē-a del cow-dhēēl-yo
The Virgin of the Pillar (12th Oct.) "America" Day	El día de la Virgen del Pilar. El día de la Hispanidad. el dēē-a day la veér-hen del pee-lár. day la ees-pa-nee-dádh
All Saints' Day (1st Nov.)	El día de Todos los Santos. el dēē-a day tó-dhos los sán-tos
The Immaculate Conception. Mother's Day.	(8th Dec.) } La Concepción. la kon-thep-thee-ón

| Christmas Eve. | La Noche Buena. |
| | la nó-chay bwáy-na |

| Christmas. | La Navidad. |
| | la na-vee-dádh |

| A Merry Christmas. | Felices Pascuas. |
| | fay-lēē-thays pás-kwas |

| A Good New Year. | Feliz Año Nuevo. |
| | fay-lēēth án-yo nwáy-vo |

| My birthday. | Mi cumpleaños. |
| | mee koom-play-án-yos |

| My saint's day. | Mi santo. |
| | mee sán-to |

TIME

VOCABULARY

afternoon, la tarde (tár-day)
evening (from about 6 p.m.), la noche (nó-chay)
hour, la hora (ó-ra)
midday, mediodía (may-dee-o-dēē-a)
midnight, medianoche (may-dee-a-nó-chay)
minute, el minuto (mee-nōō-to)
morning, la mañana (man-yá-na)
second, el segundo (say-gōōn-do)

CLOCK TIME

| What time is it? | ¿Qúe hora es? |
| | kay ó-ra es |

| It is one o'clock. | Es la una. |
| | es la ōō-na |

| It is two, three, etc., o'clock. | Son las dos, tres. . . |
| | son las dos, tres . . . |

| It is a quarter to two. | Son las dos menos cuarto. |
| | son las dos máy-nos kwár-to |

It is half past two.	Son las dos y media.
	son las dos ee máy-dee-a
At 2 a.m.	A las dos de la mañana.
	a las dos day la man-yá-na
At 2 p.m.	A las dos de la tarde.
	a las dos day la tár-day
At twenty past six.	A las seis y veinte.
	a las sáy-ees ee váy-een-tay
At about six.	A eso de las seis.
	a áy-so day las sáy-ees
It is early (late).	Es temprano (tarde).
	es taym-prá-no (tár-day)
We are early (late).	Llegamos temprano (tarde).
	lyay-gá-mos taym-prá-no (tár-day)

DAYS OF THE WEEK

day, el día (dēē-a)
week, la semana (say-má-na)
fortnight, quince días (kēēn-thay dēē-as)
Sunday, el domingo (do-mēēn-go)
Monday, el lunes (lōō-nays)
Tuesday, el martes (már-tays)
Wednesday, el miércoles (mee-ér-ko-lays)
Thursday, el jueves (hoo-áy-vays)
Friday, el viernes (vee-ér-nays)
Saturday, el sábado (sá-ba-dho)

On Sunday.	El domingo.
	el do-mēēn-go
This morning (afternoon, evening).	Esta mañana (tarde, noche).
	és-ta man-yá-na, (tár-day, nó-chay)
In the morning.	Por la mañana.
	por la man-yá-na
Tomorrow.	Mañana.
	man-yá-na

Today.	Hoy. oy
Yesterday.	Ayer. a-yér
All day.	Todo el día. tó-dho el dēē-a
Every day.	Todos los días. tó-dhos los dēē-as
The day after tomorrow.	Pasado mañana. pa-sá-dho man-yá-na
Next day.	El día siguiente. el dēē-a see-gee-én-tay
The day before yesterday.	Anteayer. an-tay a-yér-
Last week.	La semana pasada. la say-má-na pa-sá-dha
Next week.	La semana próxima. la say-má-na próx-ee-ma
Last Monday.	El lunes pasado. el lōō-nays pa-sá-dho
A working day.	Un día de trabajo. oon dēē-a day tra-bá-ho
Holidays.	Días festivos. dēē-as fes-tēē-vos

MONTHS, SEASONS AND DATES

January, enero (ay-náy-ro)
February, febrero (fay-bráy-ro)
March, marzo (már-tho)
April, abril (av-rēél)
May, mayo (má-yo)
June, junio (hōōn-yo)
July, julio (hōōl-yo)
August, agosto (a-gós-to)
September, septiembre (sep-tee-ém-bray)
October, octubre (ok-tōō-bray)
November, noviembre (no-vee-ém-bray)
December, diciembre (dee thee-ém-bray)

spring, la primavera (pree-ma-váy-ra)
summer, el verano (vay-rá-no), el estío (es-tēē-o)
autumn, el otoño (o-tón-yo)
winter, el invierno (een-vee-ér-no)
year, el año (án-yo)
month, el mes (mes)
season (of year), la estación (es-ta-thee-ón)
season (football), la temporada (tem-po-rá-dha)
holidays, las vacaciones (va-ka-thee-ó-nays)

On 1st June.   El primero de junio.
                            el pree-máy-ro day hōōn-yo

2nd June.   El dos de junio.
                            el dos day hōōn-yo

3rd June, 1965.   El tres de junio de mil novecien-
                            tos sesenta y cinco.
el tres day hōōn-yo day meel no-vay-thee-én-tos say-sén-ta ee thēēn-ko

How long have you been here? ¿ Hace cúanto tiempo que está
                            usted aquí ?
á-thay kwán-to tee-ém-po kay es-tá oos-táydh a-kēē

I have been here a few days. Hace unos pocos días que
                            estoy aquí.
á-thay ōō-nos pó-kos dēē-as kay es-tóy a-kēē

How long are you staying? ¿ Cuánto tiempo queda usted ?
                            kwán-to tee-ém-po káy-dha oos-táydh

When are you leaving?   ¿ Cuándo se marcha ?
                            kwán-do say már-cha

CORRESPONDENCE

Four model letters are provided. The first is to a Tourist Information
Bureau (to be found in many Spanish towns) requesting a list of hotels.
The second is to a hotel asking for accommodation to be reserved. Many
holiday makers, of course, do this through a travel agency. The third is
such as one might send to friends one has made in Spain. The fourth is
a short business letter. An International Reply Coupon may be bought
at any Branch Post Office.

VOCABULARY

address, las señas (sáyn-yas), la dirección (dee-rek-thee-ón)
boarding-house, la pensión (pen-see-ón)
c/o, c./de (cá-sa day)
from, desde (dés-day)
greetings, saludos (sa-lōō-dhos)
hotel, el hotel (o-tél)
inn, la posada (po-sá-dha)
management, la dirección (dee-rek-thee-ón)
manager (ess), el(la) gerente (hay-rén-tay)
Mr. (Mrs., Miss), González Sr. (Sra., Srta.) González (sen-yór, sen-yó-ra, sen-yo-rée-ta gon-thá-leth)
Mr. John (Mrs. Mary) González Sr. D. Juan (Sra. Dª. María) González (don, dón-ya)
price, el precio (práy-thee-o)
proprietor (tress), el(la) dueño(a) (doo-áyn-yo(ya)
Smith & Co. Ltd., Compañía Smith, S.A.
State tourist hotel, el parador (pa-ra-dhór)
tax, el impuesto (eem-pwés-to)
tourist bureau, la oficina de turismo (o-fee-thēē-na day too-rēēs-mo)

EXAMPLES OF LETTERS

1 THE TOURIST BUREAU
TARRAGONA
Dear Sirs,
        Would you be so kind as to send me a list of good hotels which are central (near the beach). I enclose an International Reply Coupon.
                                        Yours faithfully,

LA OFICINA DE TURISMO
TARRAGONA
Muy señores míos,
        Les ruego hagan el favor de mandarme una lista de buenos hoteles en Tarragona que estén céntricos (cerca de la playa). Va incluso con la presente un cupón de respuesta internacional.
                                        Su seguro servidor,

2 THE MANAGEMENT
THE PLAYA HOTEL
17 ST. ANTONY STREET
MÁLAGA
Dear Sirs,
        I should like to reserve one (two) single (double) room(s) (with bathroom) for 6 nights from the evening of Sunday 20th August

to the morning of Saturday 26th August, 1965. Please let me know your prices for full board (half board, accommodation only) and whether breakfast is included. I enclose an International Reply Coupon.

Yours faithfully,

La Dirección
Hotel Playa
San Antonio 17
Málaga

Muy señores míos,

Desearía reservar una (dos) habitación (-iones) con una (dos) cama(s) por 6 noches desde el domingo, 20 de agosto hasta la mañana del sábado 26 de agosto de 1965. Hagan el favor de decirme el precio de la pensión completa (la media pensión, la habitación sola) y si está incluido el desayuno. Va incluso con la presente un cupón de respuesta internacional.

Su seguro servidor,

3 My dear friend(s),

We have arrived home safely. Thank you very much for your hospitality during our stay. We shall have very pleasant memories of. . . . We hope you are all well. Give our greetings to the children. Till some other year.

Yours sincerely,

Muy estimado(s) amigo(s) mío(s),

Hemos vuelto sanos y salvos a casa. Le(s) agradecemos much-ísimo su hospitalidad durante nuestra estancia. Conservaremos un muy grato recuerdo de. . . . Esperamos que estén todos bien. Salude(n) de nuestra parte a sus hijos. Hasta otro año.

Muy cordialmente, su amigo,

García Cía. S. A.,
Catedral 127,
Madrid.

Dear Sirs,

With reference to our conversation of . . . (Refiriéndonos a nuestra conversación del . . .) We thank you for your letter (enquiry, order, offer) (Les agradecemos su carta (pregunta, pedido, ofreci-miento del . . .) We can offer you (Podemos ofrecerles). We are interested in (Nos interesa). We wish to buy (Deseamos comprar). What is the price of . . . ? (¿Qué es el precio de . . . ?) Our price is . . . (El precio es de . . .) We hope this will suit you (Esperamos que esto les convenga). Always at your service (Siempre a sus órdenes).

Yours faithfully,

(Su atento y seguro servidor,) or S.A.S.S.

FOOD, DRINKS AND RESTAURANTS

Breakfast in Spain consists of coffee or chocolate, and a bun or fritters or toasted roll with butter. Lunch time varies from about 1 p.m. in the north to 3 p.m. in the south; dinner is from about 9 p.m. in the north to 11 p.m. in the south. Should these somewhat late hours prove trying to the Anglo-Saxon stomach any tavern will provide a variety of appetisers such as prawns, squid, anchovies, eggs, cheese, crisps, olives, peanuts and roasted thrushes to see you through. Olive oil is the basis of most Spanish cooking, but only when of inferior quality need it have the alarming results sometimes reported. Those of delicate constitution may specify *con mantequilla* (kon man-tay-kēēl-ya) if they wish their meals done in butter. Spanish cooking, if sometimes a little plainer than French, is in general excellent. Here are a few well-known typical dishes:

> *Bacalao a la vizcaína* (ba-ka-lá-o a la veeth-ka-ēē-na), cod steaks in rich tomato sauce.
> *Cocido madrileño* (ko-thēē-do ma-dree-láyn-yo), boiled meat, chick-peas and potatoes
> *Cochinillo* (ko-chee-nēēl-yo), roast sucking pig
> *Gazpacho andaluz* (gath-pá-cho an-da-lōōth), cold soup: which sounds off-putting but is very refreshing
> *Paella* (pa-él-ya), fried rice, saffron, chicken, shrimps
> *Pinchitos árabes* (peen-chēē-tos á-ra-bays), highly seasoned cubes of mutton grilled over a charcoal fire

Vegetables with the exception of French fries and lettuce are normally served as a separate course, but Spaniards are noticeably unenthusiastic about greens. On the other hand a plentiful supply of delicious fruit according to season is always provided as a dessert. Contrary to common belief water is a safe and common drink with meals in Spain; it is best in the north, in Madrid and Granada. Table wines are cheap and a good local one is usually to be had. Among the better-known wine-growing districts are Rioja and Valdepeñas (ree-ó-ha; val-day-páyn-yas). On rising from table it is polite to say "*Que aproveche*" (kay a-pro-váy-chay) "Enjoy your meal" to anyone nearby still eating. The appropriate reply is "*Gracias*" (grá-thee-as): "Thank you". Finally, if wishing to sit at a table already occupied, ask permission with "*Con su permiso*" (kon soo per-mēē-so).

Spain still retains some of the vast nineteenth century cafés with mirrors, marble and venerable waiters that are unknown in Britain or the U.S.A. Here you will be served black coffee: *café solo* (ka-fáy so-lo) unless you ask for white: *con leche* (kon láy-chay), and a glass of water. Should your shoes require cleaning a shoeblack: *limpiabotas* (leem-pee-a-bó-tas) attached to the café is at your service. You may buy a lottery ticket: those on behalf of the blind: *pro ciegos* (pro thee-áy-gos) are for modest sums and are drawn every day, while the more ambitious may buy a *décimo* (dáy-thee-mo), tenth part of a ticket in the hope of winning a bigger prize. Spanish waiters are quick to spot a client, but if you wish to attract the attention of one you may either hiss or clap your hands. In the old-fashioned taverns *bodegas* (bo-dháy-gas) with their tiled walls oak beams, copper ornaments, wineskins and vats, one feels for once an atmosphere more akin to England than to France. Try a glass of draught sherry at 10 pesetas! Spanish brandies are good and very reasonably priced, as are all drinks except in night-clubs. Beer is light but pleasant.

VOCABULARY

GENERAL

aperitif, el aperitivo (a-pay-ree-tēē-vo)
appetiser, la tapa (tá-pa)
ashtray, el cenicero (thay-nee-tháy-ro)
bar, el bar (bar), el mostrador (mos-tra-dhór)
barman, el mozo del mostrador (mó-tho del mos-tra-dhór)
beer-glass, la caña (kán-ya)
bill, la cuenta (kwén-ta)
blind man, el ciego (thee-áy-go)
bottle, la botella (bo-tél-ya)
bottle, half, la media botella (máy-dhee-a bo-tél-ya)
chair, la silla (sēēl-ya)
cigar, el puro (pōō-ro)
cigarette, el cigarillo (thee-ga-rēēl-yo), el pitillo (pee-tēēl-yo)
coffee-pot, la cafetera (ka-fay-táy-ra)
cork, el corcho (kór-cho)
cork-screw, el sacacorchos (sa-ka-kór-chos)
course, el plato (plá-to)
cruet, la vinagrera (vee-na-gráy-ra)
cup, la taza (tá-tha)
dessert, el postre (pós-tray)
fork, el tenedor (tay-nay-dhór)
glass, el vaso (vá-so)
grilled, a la plancha (a la plán-cha)
hat-stand, el perchero (per-cháy-ro)
hors d'oeuvre, los entremeses (en-tray-máy-says)
hungry, to be, tener hambre (te-nér-ám-bray)
jug, el jarrito (ha-rēē-to)
knife, el cuchillo (koo-chēēl-yo)
matches, las cerillas (thay-rēēl-yas)
meal, la comida (ko-mēē-dha)
medium done, regular (ray-goo-lár)
menu, el menú (may-nōō), la lista de platos (lēēs-ta day plá-tos)
plate, el plato (plá-to)
portion, la ración (ra-thee-ón)
price, fixed, el precio fijo (pray-thēē-o fēē-ho)
restaurant, el restaurante (res-tow-rán-tay)
salad bowl, la ensaladera (en-sa-la-dháy-ra)
saucer, el platillo (pla-tēēl-yo)
self-service restaurant, el restaurante para servirse uno mismo (el res-tow-rán-tay pá-ra ser-vēēr-say ōō-no mēēs-mo)

serviette, la servilleta (ser-veel-yáy-ta)
shoeblack, el limpiabotas (leem-pee-a-bó-tas)
spoon, la cuchara (koo-chá-ra)
stew, el estofado (es-to-fá-dho), el cocido (ko-thēē-dho)
table-cloth, el mantel (man-tél)
tavern, la bodega (bo-dháy-ga)
tea-pot, la tetera (tay-táy-ra)
teaspoon, la cucharita (koo-cha-rēē-ta)
thirsty, to be, tener sed (te-nér sed)
tip, la propina (pro-pēē-na)
toothpick, el palillo (pa-lēēl-yo)
tray, la bandeja (ban-dáy-ha)
underdone, poco hecho (pó-ko áy-cho)
waiter, el camarero (ka-ma-ráy-ro)
waiter (head), el jefe de camareros (háy-fay day ka-ma-ráy-ros)
waiter(wine), el camarero de vinos (ka-ma-ráy-ro day vēē-nos)
waitress, la camarera (ka-ma-ráy-ra)
water-jug, la garrafa (ga-rá-fa)
well done, muy hecho (mwee áy-cho)
wine-glass, la copa (kó-pa)
wine-list, la lista de vinos (lēēs-ta day vēē-nos)

DRINKS

aerated water, la gaseosa (ga-say-ó-sa)
alcohol, el alcohol (al-ko-ól)
beer, la cerveza (ther-váy-tha)
brandy, el coñac (kon-yák)
burgundy, el vino de Borgoña (vēē-no day bor-gón-ya)
chocolate, el chocolate (cho-ko-lá-tay)
cider, la sidra (sēēd-ra)
claret, el clarete (kla-ráy-tay)
cocktail, el coctel (kok-tél)
coffee, black, el café solo (ka-fáy só-lo)
coffee, white, el café con leche (ka-fáy kon láy-chay)
drink, la bebida (bay-bēē-dha)
gin, la ginebra (hee-náy-bra)
ice, el hielo (ee-áy-lo)
lemonade, la limonada (lee-mo-ná-dha)
liqueurs, los licores (lee-kó-rays)
milk, la leche (láy-chay)
mineral water, el agua mineral (á-gwa mee-nay-rál)
orangeade, la naranjada (na-ran-há-dha)
port, el oporto (o-pór-to)
refreshment, el refresco (ray-frés-ko)
rum, el ron (ron)
rum and "coke", el cubalibre (koo-ba-lēē-bray)
sherry, el jerez (hay-réth)
   very dry, la manzanilla (man-than-ēēl-ya)
   dry, el jerez seco (hay-réth sáy-ko)
   medium, el amontillado (a-mon-teel-yá-dho)

brown, la solera (so-láy-ra)
siphon, el sifón (see-fón)
soda-water, el agua de seltz (ág-wa day seltz)
tea, el té (tay)
vendor, el vendedor (ven-day-dhór)
vermouth, el vermut (ver-mōōt)
water, el agua (á-gwa)
whisky, el whisky (wēēs-kay)
wine, el vino (vée-no)
    red, el vino tinto (tēēn-to)
    white, el vino blanco (blán-ko)

FOOD

anchovies, anchoas (an-chó-as)
apple, la manzana (man-thá-na)
apricot, el albaricoque (al-bar-ee-kó-kay)
artichoke, la alcachofa (al-ka-chó-fa)
asparagus, el espárrago (es-pár-ra-go)
bacon, el tocino (to-thēē-no)
banana, el plátano (plá-ta-no)
beans, French, judías (hoo-dhēē-as)
beef, la carne de vaca (kár-nay day vá-ka)
beef, roast, el rosbif (ros-bēēf)
biscuit, la galleta (gal-yáy-ta), el bizcocho (beeth-kó-cho)
brains, sesos (sáy-sos)
bread, el pan (pan)
broth, el caldo (kál-do)
butter, la mantequilla (man-tay-kēēl-ya)
cabbage, la col (kol)
cake, el pastelillo (pas-tel-ēēl-yo), la tórta (tór-ta)
carrot, la zanahoria (tha-na-ó-ree-a)
cauliflower, la coliflor (ko-lee-flór)
celery, el apio (á-pee-o)
cheese, el queso (káy-so)
chicken, el pollo (pól-yo)
chick-peas, garbanzos (gar-bán-thos)
chips, patata frita (pa-tá-ta frēē-ta)
chop, la chuleta (choo-láy-ta)
cream, la crema (kráy-ma), la nata (ná-ta)
custard, las natillas (na-tēēl-yas)
custard, cold, el flan (flan)
duck, el pato (pá-to)
egg:
    fried, un huevo al plato (oon wáy-vo al plá-to)
    boiled, un huevo pasado por agua (oon wáy-vo pa-sá-dho por á-gwa)
    hard-boiled, un huevo duro (oon wáy-vo dōō-ro)
    poached, un huevo escalfado (oon wáy-vo es-kal-fá-dho)

fish, el pescado (pes-ká-dho)
fritters, churros (chōō-ros)
fruit, la fruta (frōō-ta)
game, la caza (ká-tha)
garlic, el ajo (á-ho)
grapes, uvas (ōō-vas)
hake, la merluza (mer-lōō-tha)
ham, el jamón (ha-món)
herring, el arenque (a-rén-kay)
ice-cream, el helado (ay-lá-dho)
jam, la conserva (kon-sér-va), la mermelada (mer-may-lá-dha)
lamb, el cordero (kor-dáy-ro)
lemon, el limón (lee-món), el citrón (thee-trón)
lettuce, la lechuga (lay-chōō-ga)
lobster, la langosta (lan-gós-ta)
marmalade, la mermelada de naranja (mer-may-lá-dha day na-rán-ha)
mayonnaise, la mayonesa (ma-yo-náy-sa)
melon, el melón (may-lón)
mushrooms, setas (sáy-tas)
mussels, almejas (al-máy-has)
mustard, la mostaza (mos-tá-tha)
mutton, el carnero (kar-náy-ro)
oil, el aceite (a-tháy-ee-tay)
olives, aceitunas (a-thay-ee-tōō-nas), olivas (o-lēē-vas)
omelette: Spanish, tortilla española (tor-tēēl-ya es-pan-yó-la)
           plain, tortilla francesa (tor-tēēl-ya fran-tháy-sa)
orange, la naranja (na-rán-ha)
oysters, ostras (ós-tras)
parsley, el perejil (pay-ray-hēēl)
pastry, la pastelería (pas-tay-lay-rēē-a)
peach, el melocotón (mel-o-ko-tón)
pear, la pera (páy-ra)
peas, guisantes (gee-sán-tays)
pepper, la pimienta (pee-mee-én-ta)
pie, el pastel (pas-tél)
pimentos, pimientos (pee-mee-én-tos)
pineapple, el ananás (a-na-nás)
plums, ciruelas (thee-roo-áy-las)
pork, el cerdo (thér-do)
potato, la patata (pa-tá-ta), (la papa (pá-pa) in S. America)
   crisps, patata inglesa (pa-tá-ta een-gláy-sa)
   French fried, patata frita (pa-tá-ta frēē-ta)
poultry, la volatería (vo-la-tay-rēē-a), las aves (á-vays)
prawns, gambas (gám-bas)
radishes, rábanos (rá-ba-nos)
rice, el arroz (a-róth)
roll, el panecillo (pa-nay-thēēl-yo)
salad, la ensalada (en-sa-lá-dha)
salmon, el salmón (sal-món)

salt, la sal (sal)
sandwich, el bocadillo (bo-ka-dhēēl-yo)
sardines, sardinas (sar-dēē-nas)
  fried, boquerones (bo-kay-ró-nays)
sauce, la salsa (sál-sa)
sausage: spiced, el chorizo (cho-rēē-tho), salchichón (sal-chee-chón)
      small, la salchicha (sal-chēē-cha)
seafood, mariscos (ma-rēēs-kos)
shrimps, camarones (ka-ma-ró-nays)
snails, caracoles (ka-ra-kó-lays)
sole, el lenguado (len-gwá-dho)
soup, la sopa (só-pa)
soup, clear, el consomé (kon-so-máy)
spinach, la espinaca (es-pee-ná-ka)
squid, calamares (ka-la-má-rays)
steak, el filete (fee-láy-tay)
strawberries, fresas (fráy-sas)
sugar, el azúcar (a-thōō-kar)
tart, la tarta (tár-ta)
toast, el pan tostado (tos-tá-dho)
tomato, el tomate (to-má-tay)
trout, la trucha (trōō-cha)
vanilla, la vainilla (va-ee-nēēl-ya)
veal, la ternera (ter-náy-ra)
vegetable, la legumbre (lay-gōōm-bray), la hortaliza (or-ta-lēē-tha)
vegetable, green, la verdura (ver-dōō-ra)
vermicelli, fideos (fee-dháy-os)
whiting, el merlan (mer-lán)

Let's go for a drink.	Vamos a tomar algo. vá-mos a to-már ál-go
Let's sit down here.	Sentémonos aquí. sen-táy-mo-nos a-kēē
I am very thirsty.	Tengo mucha sed. tén-go mōō-cha sed
Be my guest.	Le convido. lay kon-vēē-dho
Two glasses of beer.	Dos cañas de cerveza. dos kán-yas day ther-váy-tha
Two glasses of brandy (sherry).	Dos copas de coñac (jerez). dos kó-pas day kon-yák (hay-réth)

Draught (bottled) beer.   Cerveza a la presión (embot-
                                    ellada).
ther-váy-tha a la pray-see-ón (em-bo-tel-yá-dha)

Stout.   Cerveza negra.
                                    ther-váy-tha náy-gra

Your health!   ¡Salud!
                                    sa-lōōdh

Waiter!   ¡Camarero!
                                    ka-ma-ráy-ro

Coming!   ¡Ya voy!
                                    ya voy

I'll buy one.   Le compro uno.
                                    lay kóm-pro ōō-no

Clean my shoes, please.   Límpieme los zapatos, por
                                    favor.
léēm-pee-ay-may los tha-pá-tos por fa-vór

Two black (white) coffees.   Dos cafés solo (con leche).
                                    dos ca-fáys só-lo (kon láy-chay)

Buttered toast.   Tostadas con mantequilla.
                                    tos-tá-dhas kon man-tay-kéēl-ya

**We are looking for a good   Buscamos un buen restaurante
(cheap) restaurant.**   (un restaurante económico).
boos-ká-mos oon boo-én res-tow-rán-tay (oon res-tow-rán-tay ay-ko-nó-mee-ko)

Can you recommend one to us?   ¿Puede usted recomendarnos
                                    uno?
poo-áy-dhay oos-táydh ray-ko-men-dár-nos ōō-no

**At what time do you serve lunch   ¿A qué hora sirven el almuerzo
(dinner)?**   (la cena)?
a kay ó-ra sēēr-ven el al-moo-ér-tho (la tháy-na)

We wish to eat.   Deseamos comer.
                                    day-say-á-mos ko-mér

**Are you serving lunch (dinner)   ¿Sirven ustedes el almuerzo
now?**   (la cena) ahora?
sēēr-ven oos-táy-dhays el al-moo-ér-tho (la tháy-na) a-ó-ra

There are six of us.   Somos seis.
                                    só-mos sáy-ees

We want to sit together.
Deseamos sentarnos juntos.
day-say-á-mos sen-tár-nos hōōn-tos

We would like to sit near the window.
Quisiéramos sentarnos junto a la ventana.
kee-see-áy-ra-mos sen-tár-nos hōōn-to a la vayn-tá-na

We do not want to sit here.
No queremos sentarnos aquí.
no kay-ráy-mos sen-tár-nos a-kēē

Where can I wash my hands?
¿Dónde puedo lavarme las manos?
dón-day poo-áy-dhay la-vár-may las mán-os

Over there. Downstairs.
Por allá. Abajo.
por al-yá. a-bá-ho

What is today's main dish?
¿Qué es el plato del día?
kay es el plá-to del dēē-a

Give me the menu, please.
Déme el menú, por favor.
dáy-may el may-nōō por fa-vór

We shall have a fixed-price meal.
Tomaremos una comida al precio fijo.
to-ma-ráy-mos ōō-na ko-mēē-dha al práy-thee-o fēē-ho

We shall order à la carte.
Pediremos a la carta.
pay-dhee-ráy-mos a la kár-ta

This ... is dirty.
Este (esta) ... está sucio(a).
és-tay (és-ta) ... es-tá sōō-thee-o(a)

I haven't a ...
No tengo ...
no tén-go ...

I do not feel like eating.
No tengo ganas de comer.
no tén-go gá-nas day ko-mér

I only want a snack.
Quiero solamente algo ligero.
kee-áy-ro so-la-mén-tay ál-go lee-háy-ro

Serve us quickly: we have to catch a train (go to the theatre).
Por favor sírvanos de prisa: tenemos que coger el tren (vamos al teatro).
por fa-vór sēēr-va-nos day prēē-sa: te-náy-mos kay ko-hér el tren (vá-mos al tay-á-tro)

We are (not) in a hurry.
(No) tenemos prisa.
no te-náy-mos prēē-sa

We want to eat right away.   Deseamos comer en seguida.
day-say-á-mos ko-mér en say-gēē-dha

What will you have to drink (as   ¿ Qué tomará usted de bebida
hors d'oeuvre, for dessert)?   (de entremeses, de postre)?
kay to-ma-rá oos-táydh day bay-bēē-dha (day en-tray-máy-says, day pós-tray)

I shall start with . . .   Para empezar tomaré . . .
pá-ra em-pe-thár to-ma-ráy

And to follow, sir?   ¿ Y para seguir, señor?
ee pá-ra say-geer, sayn-yór

Then I shall have . . .   Luego tomaré . . .
loo-áy-go to-ma-ráy . . .

What do you have in the way   ¿ Qué hay de . . . ?
of . . . ?
kay á-ee day . . .

I don't like . . .   No me gusta . . .
no me gōōs-ta . . .

I want something very simple.   Deseo algo muy sencillo.
day-sáy-o ál-go mwee sen-thēēl-yo

I'm on a diet.   Estoy al regimén.
es-tóy al ray-hee-mén

I'm not allowed to eat . . .   Me está prohibido comer . . .
may es-tá pro-ee-bēē-dho ko-mér . . .

Bring me . . .   Tráigame . . .
trá-ee-ga-may . . .

I would like steak and chips   Deseo un filete con patata frita
(ham and eggs).   (jamón y huevos al plato).
day-sáy-o oon fee-láy-tay kon pa-tá-ta frēē-ta (ha-món ee wáy-vos al plá-to)

How do you want it done?   ¿ Cómo lo quiere usted?
kó-mo lo kee-áy-ray oos-táydh

Well done (medium, underdone).   Muy hecho (regular, poco
hecho).
mwee áy-cho, (ray-goo-lár, pó-ko áy-cho)

A little more . . .   Un poco más . . .
oon pó-ko mas . . .

We are waiting to be served for the next course (for the bill, for the change).
Esperamos que nos sirvan el plato siguiente (la cuenta, el cambio).
es-pay-rá-mos kay nos sēēr-van el plá-to see-gēē-en-tay (la cwén-ta, el kám-bee-o)

I'd like a named (cheap, local) wine.
Quisiera un vino de marca (corriente, del país).
kee-see-áy-ra oon vēē-no day már-ka (ko-ree-én-tay, del pa-ēēs)

Show me the label.
Enséñeme la etiqueta.
en-sáyn-yay-may la ay-tee-káy-ta

What do you recommend?
¿Qué recomienda usted?
kay ray-ko-mee-én-da oos-táydh

This wine is corked.
Este vino está agrio.
és-tay vēē-no es-tá ág-ree-o

It doesn't smell nice.
No huele bien.
no wáy-lay bee-én

It is not very fresh.
No está muy fresco.
no es-tá mwee fráys-ko

There is too much fat.
Tiene demasiado grasa.
tee-áy-nay dee-ma-see-á-dho grá-sa

Give me a lean piece.
Démelo más magro.
dáy-may-lo mas má-gro

Do we pay you or at the desk?
¿Se lo pagamos o a la caja?
say lo pa-gá-mos o a la ká-ha

Is the service charge included?
¿Está incluido el servicio?
es-tá een-kloo-ēē-dho el ser-vēē-thee-o

Isn't there a mistake?
¿No hay error?
no á-ee ay-rór

Please check the bill again.
Sírvase volver a hacer la cuenta.
sēēr-va-say vol-vér a a-thér la kwén-ta

We didn't order ...
No pedimos ...
no pay-dhēē-mos.

That is right now.
Ahora está bien.
a-ó-ra es-tá bee-én

While I was eating someone took my . . .	Mientras comía alguien tomó mi . . .

mee-én-tras ko-mēē-a ál-gee-en to-mó mee . . .

I've left my glasses (hat, coat).	He dejado mis lentes (mi sombrero, mi abrigo).

ay day-há-dho mees lén-tays (mi som-bráy-ro, mee a-brēē-go)

We enjoyed the meal.	Nos gustó la comida.

nos goos-to la co-mēē-dha

MOTORING

While main trunk roads (*carreteras del Estado; carreteras de primer orden*) are well-maintained, this is achieved at the expense of secondary roads (*carreteras de segundo, de tercer orden*) which in some places are in a bad state and indicated as such on maps (*en mal estado*). Hair-pin bends must be expected when crossing the sierras. It is advisable to subscribe to the A.A. or R.A.C. as they provide expert advice and service to motorists intending to drive abroad, including ferry reservations, documents, repair vouchers, information on continental road signs and a manual providing detailed technical vocabulary. In any case the following documents are essential: Green Card from your Insurance Company; Temporary Exportation Certificate; International Driving Permit (for Spain, the Canaries and Balearics). Early booking is necessary for summer car ferries. There is now one operating between Southampton and Bilbao. There are no concessions in the form of petrol coupons in Spain. It is advisable to fit amber light bulbs for night driving. Police are empowered to impose fines on the spot for traffic offences. Petrol is normally sold in minimum units of ten litres.

ROAD SIGNS

Most of these are pictorial and used internationally, but here is an explanation of some of the worded signs:

¡Alto! = Halt!
Autoruta = Motorway

Calzada estrecha=Road narrows
Calzada irregular=Uneven surface
Calzada resbaladiza=Slippery surface
Ceda el paso=Give way
Cruce=Crossroads
Cuidado=Take care
Despacio=Slow
Desviación=Diversion
Dirección obligatoria=One-way traffic
Escuela=School
Estacionamiento=Parking
Glorieta=Roundabout
Obras=Road up
Pare!=Stop
Paso a nivel=Level crossing
Peligro=Danger
Prohibido adelantar=No overtaking
Prohibido el paso=No entry
Redondel=Roundabout
Salida de fábrica=Factory exit
Se prohibe estacionar=No parking

VOCABULARY

GENERAL

back, atrás (a-trás)
bend, la curva (kōōr-va)
breakdown, la avería (a-vay-rēē-a)
breakdown lorry, el coche-grúa (kó-chay-grōō-a)
bridge, el puente (pwáyn-tay)
can (petrol), el bidón (bee-dhón)
car, el coche (kó-chay), el automóvil (ow-to-mó-veel)
caravan, el coche-vivienda (kó-chay-vee-vee-én-da)
civil guard, el guardia civil (gwár-dee-a thee-vēēl)
dangerous, peligroso (pay-lee-gró-so)
drive, to, conducir (kon-dōō-theer)
driver, el conductor (kon-dook-tór)
fine, la multa (mōōl-ta)

frontier, la frontera (fron-táy-ra)
garage, el garaje (ga-rá-hay)
garage hand, el encargado (en-kar-gá-dho)
highway, la carretera (ka-ray-táy-ra)
insurance policy, la póliza de seguro (pó-lee-tha day say-gōō-ro)
left, la izquierda (eeth-kee-áyr-da)
licence, la licencia (lee-thén-thee-a)
lorry, el camión (ka-mee-ón)
mechanic, el mecánico (may-ká-nee-ko)
milestone, la piedra kilométrica (pee-áy-dra kee-lo-máy-tree-ka)
motor-cycle, la motocicleta (mo-to-thee-klάy-ta)
motorist, el motorista (mo-to-rēēs-ta), automovilista (ow-to-mo veel-ēēs-ta)
narrow, estrecho (es-tráy-cho)
number (car), la matrícula (ma-trēē-koo-la)
oil, el aceite (a-tháy-ee-tay)
patrol, la patrulla (pa-trōōl-ya)
pedestrian, el peatón (pay-a-tón)
permit, el permiso (per-mēē-so)
petrol, la gasolina (ga-so-lēē-na)
policeman, el guardia (gwár-dee-a), el policía (po-lee-thēē-a)
police-station, la comisaría (ko-mee-sa-rēē-a)
pressure, la presión (pray-see-ón)
pump (air), la bomba de aire (bóm-ba day á-ee-ray)
pump (petrol), el surtidor (soor-tee-dhór)
reverse, marcha atrás (már-cha a-trás)
right, la derecha (day-ráy-cha)
river, el río (rēē-o)
road, el camino (ka-mēē-no), la ruta (rōō-ta)
scooter, el escúter (es-kōō-ter)
service station, la estación de servicio (es-ta-thee-ón day ser-vēē thee-o)
signal, sign, la señal (sayn-yál)
signpost, el poste indicador (pós-tay een-dee-ka-dhór)
skid, to, patinar (pa-tee-nár)
spanner, la llave inglesa (lyá-vay een-gláy-sa)
spare parts, las piezas de recambio (pee-áy-thas day ray-kám-bee-o
speed limit, el límite de velocidad (lēē-mee-tay day vay-lo-thee dhádh)
straight on, adelante (a-day-lán-tay), todo seguido (tó-dho say gēē-dho)
swerve, to, desviar (des-vee-ár)
telephone, el teléfono (tay-láy-fo-no)
touring saloon, el turismo (too-rēēs-mo)
tow, to, remolcar (ray-mol-kár)
traffic jam, la obstrucción del tráfico (ob-strook-thee-ón del trá fee-ko)
traffic lights, las luces del tráfico (loó-thays del trá-fee-ko)
traffic policeman, el guardia de la circulación (gwár-dee-a day theer-koo-la-thee-ón)

trailer, el remolque (ray-mól-kay)
two-stroke mixture, la mezcla de dos tiempos (máyth-kla day dos tee-ém-pos)
vehicle, el vehículo (vay-ēē-koo-lo)
well-surfaced, en buen estado (en boo-én es-tá-dho)
wide, ancho (án-cho)

CAR

accelerator, el acelerador (a-thay-lay-ra-dhór)
battery, la batería (ba-tay-rēē-a)
body, la carrocería (kar-ro-thay-rēē-a)
bonnet, el capó (ka-pó)
boot, el maletón del equipaje (ma-lay-tón del ay-kee-pá-hay)
brake, el freno (fráy-no)
brake (hand), el freno de mano (fráy-no day má-no)
brake-lining, el forro (fór-ro)
bulb, la bombilla (bom-bēēl-ya)
bumper, el parachoques (pa-ra-chó-kays)
choke, el obturador (ob-too-ra-dhór)
clutch, el embrague (em-brá-gay)
door, la puerta (poo-áyr-ta)
exhaust, el escape (es-ká-pay)
gear box, la caja de velocidades (ká-ha day vay-lo-thee-dhá-dhays)
gear lever, la palanca de cambio (pa-lán-ka day kám-bee-o)
handle, la manivela (ma-nee-váy-la)
horn, la bocina (bo-thēē-na)
indicator, el indicador (een-dee-ka-dhór)
inner tube, la cámara de aire (ká-ma-ra day á-ee-ray)
jack, el gato (gá-to)
key, la llave (lyá-vay)
lights (head), los faros (fá-ros)
lights (side), las luces de posición (lōō-thays day po-see-thee-ón)
lights (tail), las luces de posición traseras (tra-sáy-ras)
mirror (rear-view), el espejo (retrovisor) (es-páy-ho /ray-tro-vee-sór)
nationality plate, el indicativo de nacionalidad (een-dee-ka-tēē-vo day na-thee-o-na-lee-dádh)
nut, la tuerca (too-áyr-ka)
radiator, el radiador (ra-dhee-a-dhór)
rear-window, la ventana de atrás (vayn-tá-na day a-trás)
rim, la llanta (lyán-ta)
screw, el tornillo (tor-nēēl-yo)
shock-absorber, el amortiguador (a-mor-tee-gwa-dhór)
spare wheel, la rueda de recambio (roo-áy-dha day ray-kám-bee-o)
speedometer, el cuenta-kilómetros (kwén-ta-kee-ló-may-tros)
spring, la ballesta (bal-yáys-ta)
steering, la dirección (dee-rek-thee-ón)
steering wheel, el volante (vo-lán-tay)
tank, el depósito de gasolina (day-pó-see-to day ga-so-lēē-na)

tubeless, sin cámara (seen ká-ma-ra)
tyre, el neumático (nay-oo-má-tee-ko)
washer, la arandela (a-ran-dáy-la)
wheel, la rueda (roo-áy-dha)
windscreen, el parabrisas (pa-ra-brēē-sas)
windscreen wiper, el limpia parabrisas (lēēm-pee-a pa-ra-brēē-sas)
wing, la aleta (a-láy-ta)

ENGINE

big end, la cabeza de biela (ka-báy-tha day bee-áy-la)
camshaft, el árbol de levas (ár-bol day láy-vas)
carburettor, el carburador (kar-boo-ra-dhór)
crank-case, el cárter del cigüeñal (kár-ter del thee-gwayn-yál)
crank-shaft, el árbol cigüeñal (ár-bol thee-gwayn-yál)
cylinder, el cilindro (thee-lēēn-dro)
dipstick, el indicador de nivel de aceite (een-dee-ka-dhór day nee-vél day a-tháy-ee-tay)
distributor, el distribuidor (dees-tree-bwee-dhór)
dynamo, el dínamo (dēē-na-mo)
engine, el motor (mo-tór)
fan, el ventilador (ven-tee-la-dhór)
fan-belt, la correa del ventilador (ko-ráy-a del ven-tee-la-dhór)
ignition, el encendido (en-then-dēē-dho)
piston, el pistón (pees-tón)
piston rings, los segmentos (seg-mén-tos)
plug, la bujía (boo-hēē-a)
starter, el motor de arranque (mo-tór day a-rán-kay)
valve, la válvula (vál-voo-la)

Is this the road to . . . ?   ¿Es éste el camino de . . . ?
es és-tay el ka-mēē-no day . . .

How far is it to . . . ?   ¿A cuánto de aquí está . . . ?
a kwán-to day a-kēē es-tá . . .

Which is the best road to . . . ? ¿Cuál es el mejor camino para . . . ?
kwal es el may-hór ka-mēē-no pá-ra . . .

Is it near (far)?   ¿Está cerca (lejos)?
es-tá tháyr-ka (láy-hos)

How long does it take to go ¿Cuánto se tarda en ir a . . . ?
to . . . ?
kwán-to say tár-da en eer a . . .

It is that way.	Está por allá.
	es-tá por al-yá
Go straight on.	Siga adelante. Todo seguido.
	sēē-ga a-dhay-lán-tay. tó-dho say-gēē-dho
Turn left.	Tome por la izquierda.
	tó-may por la eeth-kee-áyr-da
Turn right.	Tome por la derecha.
	tó-may por la day-ráy-cha
Go back.	Vuelva atrás.
	voo-áyl-va a-trás
Slow down.	Ande más despacio.
	án-day mas days-pá-thee-o
Stop!	¡Párese!
	pá-ray-say
Reverse!	¡Póngase en marcha atrás!
	pón-ga-say en már-cha a-trás
What is the name of this place?	¿Cómo se llama este lugar?
	kó-mo say lyá-ma és-tay loo-gár
Where is the nearest garage (telephone, restaurant, hotel)?	¿Dónde está el garaje (teléfono, restaurante, hotel) más próximo?
	dón-day es-tá el ga-rá-hay (tay-láy-fo-no, res-tow-rán-tay, o-tél) mas próx-ee-mo
You (he, she) is (are) a bad driver.	Conduce muy mal.
	kon-dōō-thay mwee mal
You were driving carelessly.	Conducía sin cuidado.
	kon-doo-thēē-a seen kwee-dhá-dho
You were going too fast.	Iba demasiado de prisa.
	ēē-ba day-ma-see-á-dho day prēē-sa
Idiot!	¡Idiota!
	ee-dhee-ó-ta
What is your name?	¿Cómo se llama usted?
	kó-mo say lyá-ma oos-táydh
	or
	¿Cuál es su nombre?
	kwál es soo nóm-bray

What is your address?   ¿Qué son sus señas?
kay son soos sáyn-yas

I didn't see ...   No vi ...
no vee ...

I didn't know.   No sabía.
no sa-bēē-a

I forgot to keep to the right.   Olvidé llevar la derecha.
ol-vee-dáy lyay-vár la day-ráy-cha

I need some petrol (air, water, oil).   Necesito gasolina (aire, agua aceite).
nay-thay-sēē-to ga-so-lēē-na (á-ee-ray, á-gwa, á-tháy-ee-tay)

Fill the tank.   Sírvase llenar el depósito.
sēēr-va-say lyay-nár el day-pó-see-to

Give me twenty litres, please.   Póngame veinte litros, po favor.
pón-ga-may váy-een-tay lēēt-ros por favór

Check the oil (battery, water).   Compruebe el aceite (la batería, el agua).
kom-proo-áy-bay el a-tháy-ēē-tay (la ba-tay-rēē-a, el á-gwa)

Check the tyres at 24 lb. per sq. in.   Compruebe los neumáticos a uno punto sesenta y nuev (kilogramos al centímetr cuadrado).
kom-proo-áy-bay los nay-oo-má-tee-kos a ōō-no pōōn-to say-sén-ta ee noo-áy-vay
(kee-lo-grá-mos al then-tēē-may-tro kwa-drá-do)
See CONVERSION TABLES pp. 143-7

Wash the windscreen (car).   Lave el parabrisas (el coche)
lá-vay el pa-ra-brēē-sas (el kó-chay)

How much is it to garage here for the night?   ¿Cuánto cobra usted si dejo e coche aquí por la noche?
kwán-to kó-bra oos-táydh se dáy-ho el kó-chay a-kēē por la nó-chay

My car is on the road two kilometres from here.   Mi coche está en la ruta a do kilómetros de aquí.
mee kó-chay es-tá en la rōō-ta a dos kee-ló-may-tros day a-kēē

| My car has broken down. | Mi coche está con averías. |
| | mee kó-chay es-tá con a-vay-rēē-as |

| My car will not start. | Mi coche no arranca. |
| | mee kó-chay no ar-rán-ka |

| I have had a puncture. | He tenido un pinchazo. |
| | ay tay-nēē-dho oon peen-chá-tho |

| The battery is run down. | La batería no funciona. |
| | la ba-tay-rēē-a no foon-thee-ó-na |

| There is something wrong. | Hay algo que no anda. |
| | á-ee ál-go kay no án-da |

| Can you send someone? | ¿Puede usted mandar a alguien? |
| | poo-áy-dhay oos-táydh man-dár a ál-gee-en |

| Can you tow it? | ¿Puede usted remolcarlo? |
| | poo-áy-dhay oos-táydh ray-mol-kár-lo |

| Does the carburettor need cleaning? | ¿Hay que limpiar el carburador? |
| | á-ee kay leem-pee-ár el kar-boo-ra-dhór |

| What is wrong? | ¿Qué pasa? |
| | kay pá-sa |

| . . . is broken (loose). | . . . está roto (flojo). |
| | . . . es-tá ró-to (fló-ho) |

| The brakes need adjusting. | Hay que ajustar los frenos. |
| | á-ee kay a-hoos-tár los fráy-nos |

| There is a leak. | Hay un escape. |
| | á-ee oon es-ká-pay |

| This must be replaced (straightened, repaired). | Hay que reemplazar (enderezar, arreglar) esto. |
| | á-ee kay ray-em-pla-thár (en-dhay-ray-thár, ar-ray-glár) és-to |

| How long will it take? | ¿Cuánto tiempo necesitará? |
| | kwán-to tee-ém-po nay-thay-see-ta-rá |

| Can't you do it at once? | ¿No puede usted hacerlo en seguida? |
| | no poo-áy-dhay oos-táydh a-thér-lo en say-gēē-dha |

| How much will the repair cost? | ¿Cuánto costará arreglarlo? |
| | kwán-to kos-ta-rá ar-ray-glár-lo |

When can I collect it? ¿ Cuándo puedo recogerlo ?
kwán-do poo-áy-dho ray-ko-hér-lo

Can you lend me ... ? ¿ Puede usted prestarme ... ?
poo-áy-dhay oos-táydh pres-tár-may ...

I want to hire a car. Deseo alquilar un coche.
day-sáy-o al-kee-lár oon kó-chay

How much is it per hour (per day)? ¿ Cuánto es por hora (al día)?
kwán-to es por ó-ra (al dēē-a)

TRAVEL

CUSTOMS AND PORTERS

Travellers to Spain should ascertain (from a consulate, passport office
or a travel agency) whether a certificate of vaccination against smallpox
will be required; if so they should obtain a form from their local health
authority to take to their doctor. As a concession small amounts of alcohol
and tobacco may be brought in if for personal use, carried in one's hand
luggage and declared. It is as well to check on this with, for instance, the
duty-free shops at airports. One must be present when the Customs check
one's luggage and have keys ready. If a porter is employed, note his number
to be sure of identifying him. Personal trolleys may be available at airports.
One should make a list of all purchases whether liable to duty or not and
declare them when returning to Britain. Here again small concessions are
made subject to the same conditions as above. Keep a receipt of purchase
of any fairly expensive article.

VOCABULARY

alcohol, el alcohol (al-ko-ól)
bag, el saco (sá-ko)
bank-note, el billete de banco (beel-yáy-tay day bán-ko)
bottle, la botella (bo-táyl-ya)
box, la caja (ká-ha)
camera, la máquina fotográfica (má-kee-na fo-to-grá-fee-ka)
cigar, el puro (pōō-ro)
cigarette, el cigarillo (thee-ga-rēēl-yo)
Customs, la Aduana (ad-wá-na)
customs officer, el aduanero (ad-wa-náy-ro)

key, la llave (lyá-vay)
label, la etiqueta (ay-tee-káy-ta)
luggage, el equipaje (ay-kee-pá-hay)
money, el dinero (dee-náy-ro)
number, el número (nōō-may-ro)
porter, el mozo (mó-tho)
passport, el pasaporte (pa-sa-pór-tay)
present, el regalo (ray-gá-lo)
suitcase, la maleta (ma-láy-ta)
tobacco, el tabaco (ta-bá-ko)
train, el tren (tren)
traveller's cheque, el cheque de viajero (cháy-kay day vee-a-háy-ro)
trunk, el baúl (ba-ōōl)

Carry this please.	Lléveme esto por favor. lyáy-vay-may és-to por fa-vór
What is your number?	¿Qué número tiene? kay nōō-may-ro tee-áy-nay
That is all.	Es todo. es tó-dho
I shall take this myself.	Tomaré esto yo mismo. to-ma-ráy és-to yo mís-mo
I'll keep my hand luggage.	Voy a guardar mi equipaje de mano. voy a gwar-dár mee ay-kee-pá-hay day má-no.
Careful with that!	¡Cuidado con eso! kwee-dá-dho con áy-so
There's another bag there.	Hay otro saco allí. á-ee ó-tro sá-ko al-yēē
Don't leave this!	¡No deje esto! No dáy-hay és-to
Don't forget that!	¡No olvide eso! no ol-vēē-dhay áy-so
I can't find my porter.	No encuentro a mi mozo. no en-kwén-tro a mee mó-tho
Have you seen porter number ten?	¿Ha visto usted al mozo número diez? a vēēs-to oos-táydh al mó-tho nōō-may-ro dee-éth

What do I owe you for three items? ¿Qué le debo por los tres bultos?
kay lay dáy-bo por los tres bōōl-tos

Have you anything to declare? ¿Tiene usted algo que declarar?
tee-áy-nay oos-táydh ál-go kay day-kla-rár

Only some presents. Solamente algunos regalos.
so-la-mén-tay al-gōō-nos ray-gá-los

I only have this. No tengo más que esto.
no tén-go mas kay és-to

No alcohol (tobacco). Ningún alcohol (tabaco).
neen-gōōn al-ko-ól (ta-bá-ko)

Some alcohol (tobacco). Algún alcohol (tabaco)
al-gōōn al-ko-ól (ta-bá-ko)

It's for my personal use. Es para mi uso personal.
es pá-ra mee oó-so per-so-nál

I've nothing to declare. No tengo nada que declarar.
no tén-go ná-da kay day-kla-rár

Anything else? ¿Otra cosa?
ó-tra kó-sa

It's already marked. Ya está señalado.
ya es-tá sayn-ya-lá-dho

Open it please! ¡Abralo por favor!
á-bra-lo por fa-vór

You must pay duty. Usted debe pagar los derechos.
oos-táydh dáy-bay pa-gár los day-ráy-chos

This way please. Por aquí, haga el favor.
por a-kēē, á-ga el fa-vór

Where is the way out? ¿Dónde está la salida?
dón-day es-tá la sa-lēē-dha

It's been used. Es usado.
es oo-sá-dho

Have you any Spanish (English) money? ¿Tiene usted dinero español (inglés)?
tee-áy-nay oos-táydh dee-náy-ro es-pan-yól (een-gláys)

I have some notes (traveller's cheques).	Tengo algunos billetes (cheques de viajero).

tén-go al-gōō-nos beel-yáy-tays (chay-káys day vee-a-háy-ro)

Please move on.	Pase usted por favor.

pá-say oos-táydh por fa-vór

TRAINS

Spanish Railways (*la Red Nacional de Ferrocarriles Españoles* or R.N.F.E. for short, pronounced rén-fay) have to contend with mountainous terrain often using ageing rolling stock. This sometimes results in slow travel especially in the case of the *correo* (mail-train) and *ómnibus* (stopping-train). On the other hand the T.A.L.G.O., a fast first-class express on which a supplement is payable, runs on main lines. On ordinary express trains *rápido* or *expreso*, 3rd class is uncomfortable but rich in local colour, 2nd class is quite comfortable and 1st not appreciably more so. Restaurant-cars provide excellent meals at prices which compare well with other European railways. It is customary to take a basket of food for one's journey. This can be supplemented from station buffets and vendors. A variety of food is quite likely to be pressed on the traveller who has not started on his own supply. If such generosity becomes overwhelming a polite refusal would be *Gracias, que aproveche* (grá-thee-as kay ap-ro-váy-chay), No thanks, but may you enjoy it.

Trains are usually full, so one should book a seat in advance. In large towns there is often a central R.N.F.E. office where this may be done. In smaller towns it is advisable, about 1½ hours before the time of departure, to get a porter to buy your ticket and secure your seat. This method is perfectly reliable and will save a tedious wait with uncertain prospects as the ticket office sells tickets for only an hour before departure time. Allow a tip of 10% of the fare. Rail travel in Spain is an excellent way of getting to know the people as they are very ready to take a polite interest in their fellow passengers.

VOCABULARY

arrival, la llegada (lyay-gá-dha)
back to engine, de espalda a la máquina (day es-pál-da a la má-kee-na)
berth, la cama (ká-ma), la litera (lee-táy-ra)
blanket, la manta (mán-ta)
blind, la persiana (payr-see-á-na)
booking-office, el despacho de billetes (days-pá-cho day beel-yáy-tays)
bookstall, el puesto de periódicos (pwáys-to day pay-ree-ó-dhee-kos)
buffet bar, la cantina (kan-tēē-na)
carriage, el coche (kó-chay), el vagón (va-gón)
compartment, el departamento (day-par-ta-mén-to)

S.P.B.----C

communication cord, el timbre de alarma (tēēm-bray day a-lár-ma)
connection, el empalme (em-pál-may)
corner, el rincón (reen-kón)
corridor, el pasillo (pa-sēēl-yo)
delay, el retraso (ray-trá-so)
departure, la salida (sa-lēē-dha)
dining-car, el coche-restaurante (kó-chay-res-tow-rán-tay)
dinner, la cena (tháy-na)
door, la portezuela (por-tay-thoo-áy-la)
draught, la corriente de aire (ko-ree-én-tay day á-ee-ray)
engine, la máquina (má-kee-na), la locomotora (lo-ko-mo-tó-ra)
enquiry office, la oficina de informaciones (o-fee-thēē-na day een-for-ma-thee-ó-nays)
entrance, la entrada (ayn-trá-dha)
exit, la salida (sa-lēē-dha)
facing the engine, de cara a la máquina (day ká-ra a la má-kee-na)
fare, el precio del viaje (práy-thee-o del vee-á-hay)
first class, de primera clase (day pree-máy-ra klá-say)
gentlemen, caballeros (ka-bal-yáy-ros)
guard, el jefe de tren (háy-fay day tren)
guard's van, el furgón de equipajes (foor-gón dey ay-kee-pá-hays)
journey, el viaje (vee-á-hay), el trayecto (tra-yáyk-to)
ladies, señoras (sayn-yó-ras)
lavatory, el retrete (ray-tráy-tay)
left-luggage, la consigna (kon-sēēn-ya)
luggage, el equipaje (ay-kee-pá-hay)
luggage-ticket, el talón (ta-lón)
lunch, el almuerzo (al-moo-ér-tho)
newspaper, el periódico (pay-ree-ó-dhee-ko)
number, el numero (nōō-may-ro)
occupied, ocupado (o-koo-pá-dho)
passenger, el viajero (vee-a-háy-ro)
pillow, la almohada (al-mo-á-dha)
place, el sitio (sēē-tee-o)
platform, el andén (an-dén)
porter, el mozo (mó-tho)
rack, la red (raydh)
railway, el ferrocarril (fay-ro-ka-rēēl)
seat, el asiento (a-see-én-to)
second class, de segunda clase (day say-gōōn-da klá-say)
sleeping-car, el coche-camas (kó-chay-ká-mas)
smokers, fumadores (foo-ma-dhó-rays)
station, la estación (es-ta-thee-ón)
station-master, el jefe de estación (háy-fay day es-ta-thee-ón)
subway, el corredor subterráneo (ko-ray-dhór soob-tay-rá-nay-o)
suitcase, la maleta (ma-láy-ta)
supplement, el suplemento (soo-play-mén-to)
third class, de tercera clase (day ter-tháy-ra klá-say)
ticket, el billete (beel-yáy-tay)
ticket inspector, el revisor (ray-vee-sór)

ticket (return), el billete de ida y vuelta (day ēē-dha ee voo-áyl-ta)
time-table, el horario (o-rá-ree-o)
vacant, libre (lēē-bray)
valid, válido (vá-lee-dho)
waiting-room, la sala de espera (sá-la day es-páy-ra)
window (of carriage), la ventanilla (vayn-ta-nēēl-ya)
window (of booking office), la taquilla (ta-kēēl-ya)

What is the fare to . . . ?	¿ Qué es el precio del viaje a . . ?
	kay es el práy-thee-o del vee-á-hay a . . .

I should like to reserve a first   Quisiera reservar un asiento de
(second) class seat.   primera (segunda) clase.
kee-see-áy-ra ray-ser-vár oon a-see-én-to day pree-máy-ra (say-gōōn-da) klá-say

I have two seats reserved.   Tengo reservados dos asientos.
tén-go ray-ser-vá-dhos dos a-see-én-tos

Find me a corner seat by the   Búsqueme   un   asiento   de
window.   rincón junto a la ventanilla.
bōōs-kay-may oon a-see-én-to day reen-kón hōōn-to a la ven-ta-nēēl-ya

Are there any vacant berths in ¿ Hay   plazas   en   el   coche-
the sleeping-car?   camas?
á-ee plá-thas en el kó-chay-ká-mas

Is there a dining-car on this   ¿ Hay un coche-restaurante en
train?   este tren?
á-ee oon kó-chay-res-tow-rán-tay en és-tay tren

I have reserved a sleeper.   He reservado una litera.
ay ray-ser-vá-dho ōō-na lee-táy-ra

Is it free?   ¿ Está libre?
es-tá lēē-bray

It is occupied (reserved).   Está ocupado (reservado).
es-tá o-koo-pá-dho (ray-ser-vá-dho)

I believe it is my seat.   Creo que es mi asiento.
kráy-o kay es mee a-see-én-to

Where is the guard (ticket   ¿ Dónde está el jefe de tren
inspector)?   (el revisor)?
dón-day es-tá el háy-fay day tren (el ray-vēē-sor)

Find me another seat!   ¡Búsqueme otro asiento!
bōōs-kay-may ó-tro a-see-én-to

Nearer the dining-car.   Más cerca del coche-restaurante.
mas thér-ka del kó-chay-res-tow-rán-tay

I shall pay the excess.   Pagaré el suplemento.
pa-ga-ráy el soo-play-mén-to

When does the train leave for ... ?   ¿A qué hora sale el tren para ... ?
a kay ó-ra sá-lay el tren pá-ra ...

When does it arrive at ... ?   ¿Cuándo llega a ... ?
kwán-do lyáy-ga a ...

Is there a through train to ... ?   ¿Hay un tren directo a ... ?
á-ee oon tren dee-rék-to a ...

Must I change for ... ?   ¿Debo cambiar para ... ?
dáy-bo kam-bee-ár pá-ra ...

Where must I get off for ... ?   ¿Dónde debo bajar para ... ?
dón-day dáy-bo ba-hár pá-ra

Where can I buy a platform ticket?   ¿Dónde puedo comprar un billete de andén?
dón-day pwáy-dho kom-prár oon beel-yáy-tay day an-dén

Is there a reduced fare for children?   ¿Hay una tarifa reducida para los niños?
á-ee oó-na ta-rēē-fa ray-doo-theé-dha pá-ra los nēēn-yos

It is not valid.   No vale.
no vá-lay

I want to register this for ...   Deseo facturar esto para ...
day-sáy-o fak-too-rár áys-to pá-ra ...

Please give me a receipt.   Por favor déme un recibo.
por fa-vór dáy-may oon ray-thēē-bo

Is this the right train for ... ?   ¿Es en efecto el tren para ... ?
es en ay-fék-to el tren pá-ra ...

May I put my case here?   ¿Permite usted que ponga mi maleta aquí?
per-mēē-tay oos-táydh kay pón-ga mee ma-láy-ta a-kēē

All aboard!   ¡Señores viajeros, al tren!
sayn-yó-rays vee-a-háy-ros, al tren

May I open (close) the window?   ¿Permite usted que abra (cierre) la ventanilla?

per-mēē-tay oos-táydh kay áb-ra (thee-áy-ray) la vayn-ta-nēēl-ya

Where is the toilet?   ¿Dónde está el retrete?

dón-day es-tá el ray-tráy-tay

I have left my ticket in the compartment.   He dejado mi billete en el departamento.

ay day-há-dho mee beel-yáy-tay en el day-par-ta-mén-to

When do we get to . . . ?   Cuándo llegamos a . . . ?

kwán-do lyay-gá-mos a . . .

At what time is the first (second) service?   ¿A qué hora es el primer (segundo) servicio?

a kay ó-ra es el pree-mér (say-gōōn-do) ser-vēē-thee-o

At the front (back) of the train.   A la cabeza del (a la cola del) tren.

a la ka-báy-tha del (a la kó-la del) tren

How much late are we running?   ¿Cuánto de retraso llevamos?

kwán-to day ray-trá-so lyay-vá-mos

We are running ten minutes late.   Llevamos diez minutos de retraso.

lyay-vá-mos dee-éth mee-nōō-tos day ray-trá-so

We will arrive on time.   Llegaremos a la hora.

lyay-ga-ráy-mos a la ó-ra

How long does the train stop here?   ¿Cuánto para el tren aquí?

kwán-to pá-ra el tren a-kēē

Do we pass through . . . ?   ¿Pasamos por . . . ?

pa-sá-mos por . . .

Do you smoke?   ¿Fuma usted?

fōō-ma oos-táydh

Would you like to read my paper?   ¿Desea usted leer mi periódico?

day-sáy-a oos-táydh lay-ér mee pay-ree-ó-dee-ko

Do you mind if I smoke?   ¿Le molesta que yo fume?

lay mo-lés-ta kay yo fōō-may

Where is the left-luggage office? ¿Dónde está la consigna?
dón-day es-tá la con-sēēn-ya

I want to leave this luggage. Deseo dejar este equipaje.
day-sáy-o day-hár és-tay ay-kee-pá-hay

I shall come for them this afternoon (evening). Vendré a cogerlas esta tarde (noche).
ven-dráy a ko-hér-las és-ta tár-day (nó-chay)

I am leaving by the nine o'clock train. Me marcho con el tren de las nueve.
may már-cho kon el tren day las noo-áy-vay

I want to take out my luggage. Deseo sacar mi equipaje.
day-sáy-o sa-kár mee ay-kee-pá-hay

Here is my luggage ticket. Aquí tiene usted mi talón.
a-kēē tee-áy-nay oos-táydh mee ta-lón

This is not mine. Esto no es mío.
és-to no es mēē-o

Where is the lost property office? ¿Dónde está la oficina de objetos perdidos?
dón-day es-tá la o-fee-thēē-na day ob-háy-tos per-dēē-dhos

There is a case missing. Falta una maleta.
fál-ta ōō-na ma-láy-ta

I've got into the wrong train. Me he equivocado de tren.
may ay ay-kee-vo-ká-dho day tren

I've missed the train to . . . He perdido el tren de . . .
ay per-dhēē-dho el tren day . . .

How long shall I have to wait? ¿Cuánto tiempo tendré que esperar?
kwán-to tee-ém-po ten-dráy kay es-pay-rár

The last train has gone. El último tren ha salido.
el ōōl-tee-mo tren a sa-lēē-dho

PLANE

B.E.A. in co-operation with Iberia Air Lines of Spain and Gibair, provide scheduled flights to Madrid, Barcelona, Gibraltar, Málaga, Mallorca, the Canaries, Tangier and Valencia. Other places in Spain are served by Iberia and, in season, by chartered flights. At London airport a service charge is payable when embarking on an international flight. The free baggage allowance is: Tourist class 44 lb. (20 kg.), First class 66 lb. (30 kg.). Excess baggage must be paid for at rates varying with the distance. The London Air Terminal is situated in Cromwell Road, S.W.7.

At the time of going to press B.U.A. plan flights to Madrid, Las Palmas, Buenos Aires, Montevideo and Santiago.

VOCABULARY

aeroplane, el avión (a-vee-ón)
air hostess, la azafata (a-tha-fá-ta)
airline, la línea aérea (lēē-nay-a a-áy-ray-a)
air-pocket, el bache (bá-chay)
airsick, mareado (ma-ray-á-dho)
air terminal, el aeropuerto terminal (a-ay-ro-poo-áyr-to ter-mee-nál)
arm-rest, el brazo (brá-tho)
ashtray, el cenicero (thay-nee-tháy-ro)
cloud, la nube (nōō-bay)
cotton-wool, el algodón (al-go-dhón)
crew, la tripulación (tree-poo-la-thee-ón)
emergency exit, la salida de socorro (sa-lēē-da day so-kó-ro)
engine, el motor (mo-tór)
flight, el vuelo (voo-áy-lo)
fog, la niebla (nee-áy-bla)
jet aircraft, el avión de reacción (a-vee-ón day ray-ak-thee-ón)
land, to, aterrizar (a-tay-ree-thár)
paper bag, el saco de papel (sá-ko day pa-pél)
passenger, el viajero (vee-a-háy-ro)
pill, la píldora (pēēl-do-ra)
pilot, el piloto (pee-ló-to)
propeller, la hélice (áy-lee-thay)
refreshment, el refresco (ray-frés-ko)
runway, la pista de aterrizaje (pēēs-ta day a-tay-ree-thá-hay)
safety-belt, el cinturón de seguridad (theen-too-rón day say-goo-ree-dhádh)
steward, el camarero (ka-ma-ráy-ro)
stewardess, la camarera (ka-ma-ráy-ra)
storm, la borrasca (bo-rás-ka), la tormenta (tor-mén-ta)
sweet, el caramelo (ka-ra-máy-lo)
take off, to, despegar (des-pay-gár)
tray, la bandeja (ban-dáy-ha)
turbo-jet, el turborreactor (toor-bo-ray-ak-tór)
weather forecast, el pronóstico meteorológico (pro-nós-tee-ko may-tay-o-ro-ló-hee-ko)
window, la ventanilla (vayn-ta-nēēl-ya)
wing, el ala (*f.*) (á-la)

Where are the airline offices? ¿Dónde están las oficinas de la línea aérea?

dón-day es-tán las o-fee-thēē-nas day la lēē-nay-a a-áy-ray-a

When is the plane to ... ? ¿Cuándo hay avión a ... ?

kwán-do á-ee a-vee-ón a ...

What is the fare? ¿Cuánto es el billete?

kwán-to es el beel-yáy-tay

Tourist class. De segunda clase.

day say-gōōn-da klá-say

First class. De primera clase.

day pree-máy-ra klá-say

Return. De ida y vuelta.

day ēē-dha ee voo-áyl-ta

How do I get to the airport (air terminal)? ¿Cómo se va al aeropuerto (al aeropuerto terminal)?

kó-mo say va al a-ay-ro-poo-áyr-to (a-ay-ro-poo-áyr-to ter-mee-nál)

I want to reserve a seat on the plane leaving on Thursday for ... Deseo reservar un asiento en el avión que sale el jueves para ...

day-sáy-o ray-ser-vár oon a-see-én-to en el a-vee-ón kay sá-lay el hoo-áy-vays pá-ra ...

Is there a bus to the airport? ¿Hay un autocar hasta el aeropuerto?

á-ee oon ow-to-kár ás-ta el a-ay-ro-poo-áyr-to

Can I change my seat? ¿Puedo cambiar de asiento?

pwáy-do kam-bee-ár day a-see-én-to

Would you like some refreshment? ¿Desea usted algún refresco?

day-sáy-a oos-táydh al-gōōn ray-frés-ko

I should like some coffee (brandy). Quisiera café (coñac).

kee-see-áy-ra ka-fáy (kon-yák)

I am feeling sick. Estoy mareado.

es-tóy ma-ray-á-dho

ive me a paper bag (glass of water).
Déme un saco de papel (un vaso de agua).
dáy-may oon sá-ko day pa-pél (oon vá-so day á-gwa)

here is the toilet?
¿Dónde está el excusado?
dón-day es-tá el ex-koo-sá-dho

elcome aboard.
Sean los bienvenidos a bordo.
sáy-an los bee-en-ven-ēē-dos a bór-do

he sky is clear (cloudy).
El cielo está despejado (nublado).
el thee-áy-lo es-tá days-pay-há-dho (noo-blá-dho)

e shall be flying at a height of 12,000 feet.
Volaremos a una altura de cuatro mil metros.
vo-la-ráy-mos a ōō-na al-tōō-ra day kwá-tro meel máy-tros

e shall run into some disturbance.
Encontraremos una borrasca.
en-kon-tra-ráy-mos ōō-na bo-rás-ka

here is fog at Barcelona.
Hay niebla en Barcelona.
á-ee nee-áy-bla en bar-thay-ló-na

ould passengers on flight 10 to Barcelona please go to door A.
Se ruega a los viajeros del vuelo número diez a Barcelona que pasen a la puerta A.
y roo-áy-ga a los vee-a-háy-ros del voo-áy-lo nōō-may-ro dee-éth a bar-thay-ló-na kay pá-sen a la pwáyr-ta a

he plane from Palma is arriving.
Se anuncia la llegada del vuelo de Palma.
say a-nōōn-thee-a la lyay-gá-dha del voo-áy-lo day pál-ma

e are crossing over the Spanish coast.
Estamos cruzando por encima de la costa española.
es-tá-mos kroo-thán-do por en-thēē-ma day la kós-ta es-pan-yó-la

e shall be landing in five minutes.
Aterrizaremos dentro de cinco minutos.
a-tay-ree-tha-ráy-mos dén-tro day thēēn-ko mee-nōō-tos

lease fasten your safety-belts and put out your cigarettes.
Sírvanse abrochar su cinturón de seguridad y apagar los cigarillos.
sēēr-van-say a-bro-chár soo theen-too-rón day say-goo-ree-dhádh ee a-pa-gár los thee-ga-rēēl-yos

You may smoke if you wish but   Pueden fumar si quieren, pe
cigarettes only please.   solamente los cigarillos p
             favor.

poo-áy-den foo-már see kee-áy-ren, pé-ro so-la-mén-tay los thee-ga-rĕĕl-yos
por fa-vór

COACH, BUS, TRAM, TAXI

In some areas travel by long-distance coach is faster and more comforta
than by train. One disadvantage is the early hour of departure, often 6 a.
Bus and tram fares in town are cheap. Sometimes the driver collects far
sometimes the conductor sits at a ticket machine. Often one boards
vehicle at one end and gets off at the other. Spaniards, who are po
people on other occasions, have an aversion to queueing. Taxi fares
very reasonable, but there are the usual extra charges for luggage,
travel outwith town boundaries or for journeys late at night.

VOCABULARY

bus (town), el autobús (ow-to-bōōs)
bus (touring), el autocar (ow-to-kár)
bus stop, la parada (pa-rá-dha)
change, el dinero suelto (dee-náy-ro swáyl-to)
change, to, cambiar (kam-bee-ár)
coach, el coche de línea (kó-chay day lēē-nay-a)
conductor, el cobrador (ko-bra-dhór)
driver, el conductor (kon-dook-tór), el chófer (chó-fer)
front-seat, la delantera (day-lan-táy-ra)
half-fare, el medio billete (máy-dee-o beel-yáy-tay)
platform, la plataforma (pla-ta-fór-ma)
route, el recorrido (ray-ko-rēē-dho)
taxi, el taxi (ták-see)
taxi-driver, el chófer de taxi (chó-fer day ták-see)
terminus, el fin del recorrido (feen del ray-ko-rēē-dho)
tip, la propina (pro-pēē-na)
tram, el tranvía (tran-bēē-a)
trolleybus, el trolebús (tro-lay-bōōs)

Where can I catch a bus to ... ?   ¿Dónde puedo coger un aut
                   bús a ... ?

dón-day pwáy-dho ko-her oon ow-to-bōōs a ...

want to buy a bus ticket to . . .
Deseo comprar un billete de autocar para . . .
day-sáy-o kom-prár oon beel-yáy-tay day ow-to-kár pá-ra . . .

here does the coach to . . . leave from?
¿De dónde sale el coche de . . . ?
day dón-day sá-lay el kó-chay day . . .

t what time does it leave?
¿A qué hora sale?
a kay ó-ra sá-lay

haven't any change.
No tengo dinero suelto.
no tén-go dee-náy-ro swáyl-to

love right forward please!
¡Pasen adelante por favor!
pá-sen a-dhay-lán-tay por fa-vór

verybody off (all change)!
¡Que baje (cambie) todo el mundo!
kay bá-hay (kám-bee-ay) tó-dho el mōōn-do

an you tell me where to get off for . . . ?
¿Puede usted decirme dónde bajar para . . . ?
pwáy-dhay oos-táydh day-thēēr-may dón-day ba-hár pá-ra . . .

on't forget to tell me.
No olvide decírmelo.
no ol-vēē-dhay day-thēēr-may-lo

et off at the next stop.
Baje usted a la parada siguiente.
bá-hay oos-táydh a la pa-rá-dha see-gee-én-tay

should like a front seat (seat near the window).
Quisiera una delantera (un asiento cerca de la ventana).
kee-see-áy-ra ōō-na day-lan-táy-ra (oon a-see-én-to tháyr-ka day la vayn-tá-na)

he bus will stop here for half an hour.
El coche parará aquí por media hora.
el kó-chay pa-ra-rá a-kēē por máy-dee-a ó-ra

ake me to the station!
¡Lléveme a la estación!
Lyáy-vay-may a la es-ta-thee-ón

m in a hurry.
Tengo prisa.
tén-go prēē-sa

ve a train to catch.
Tengo que coger un tren.
tén-go kay ko-hér oon tren

on't go so fast!
¡No vaya tan de prisa!
no vá-ya tan day prēē-sa

Stop here! ¡Párese aquí!
pá-ray-say a-kēē

Wait here! ¡Espere aquí!
es-páy-ray a-kēē

Come and collect us at eight Venga a recogernos a las och
o'clock tomorrow morning. mañana por la mañana.
váyn-ga a ray-ko-hér-nos a las óch-o man-yá-na por la man-yá-na

SHIP

aft, hacia popa (á-thee-a pó-pa)
berth, la litera (lee-táy-ra)
boat, el barco (bár-ko)
bridge, el puente de mando (poo-én-tay day mán-do)
cabin, el camarote (ka-ma-ró-tay)
crossing, la travesía (tra-vay-sēē-a)
deck, la cubierta (koo-bee-áyr-ta)
deck-chair, la silla de cubierta (sēēl-ya)
disembark, to, desembarcar (des-em-bar-kár)
embark, to, embarcarse (em-bar-kár-say)
ferry, el pasaje (pa-sá-hay)
forward, hacia proa (á-thee-a pró-a)
gangway, el pasamano (pa-sa-má-no)
harbour, el puerto (poo-áyr-to)
ladder, la escalera (es-ka-láy-ra)
landing ticket, el billete de desembarco (beel-yáy-tay d
des-em-bár-ko)
lifeboat, el bote salvavidas (bó-tay sal-va-vēē-dhas)
life-jacket, el chaleco salvavidas (cha-láy-ko sal-va-vēē-dha
port (side), babor (bá-bor)
port (harbour), el puerto (poo-áyr-to)
purser's office, la oficina del contador (o-fee-thēē-na
kon-ta-dhór)
quay, el muelle (moo-él-yay)
starboard, estribor (es-trēē-bor)
yacht, el yate (yá-tay)

Which is the way to the harbour ¿Por dónde está el puerto
(wharf)? muelle)?
por dón-day es-tá el poo-áyr-to (el moo-áyl-yay)

ow long does the crossing take? ¿ Cuánto dura la travesía?
kwán-to dōō-ra la tra-vay-sēē-a

want a first (second) class cabin (berth). Deseo un camarote (una litera) de primera (segunda) clase.
day-sáy-o oon ka-ma-ró-tay (ōō-na lee-táy-ra) day pree-máy-ra (say-gōōn-da) klá-say

hen does the boat leave for ...? ¿ Cuándo sale el barco para ...?
kwán-do sá-lay el bár-ko pá-ra .

hen does the boat arrive at ...? ¿ Cuándo llega el barco a ...?
kwán-do lyáy-ga el bár-ko a ...

oes it call at ...? ¿ Hace escala en ...?
á-thay es-ká-la en .

here is the saloon (bar)? ¿ Dónde está el salón (bar)?
dón-day es-tá el sa-lón (bar)

here do I get a landing-ticket? ¿ Dónde se sacan los billetes de desembarco?
dón-day say sá-kan los beel-yáy-tays day des-em-bár-ko

want a deck-chair. Deseo una silla de cubierta.
day-sáy-o ōō-na sēēl-ya day koo-bee-áyr-ta

am sea-sick. Estoy mareado.
es-tóy ma-ray-á-dho

ave you any sea-sickness pills? ¿ Tiene usted píldoras contra el mareo?
tee-áy-nay oos-táydh pēēl-do-ras kón-tra el ma-ráy-o

ring me a basin! ¡Tráigame una jofaina!
trá-ee-ga-may ōō-na ho-fá-ee-na

ow long can we stay ashore? ¿ Cuánto tiempo podemos quedar en tierra?
kwán-to tee-ém-po po-dháy-mos kay-dár en tee-áyr-ra

old on tight! ¡Agárrese bien!
a-gár-ray-say bee-én

ind your head! ¡Cuidado con la cabeza!
kwee-dhá-dho kon la ka-bé-tha

HOTELS

These are classified by the Ministry of Tourism from Luxury to Thi
Class. There are also *paradores* often in renovated buildings of historic
interest and *albergues* similar to motels, which are government-own
and lists of which may be obtained from the National Tourist Offic
Higher rates are charged for a stay of only two days than for a longer peri
and also at busy times, for example Holy Week in Seville. Meals are serv
progressively later as one goes south: lunch in the north at about 1 p.
but as late as 3 p.m. in the south; dinner in the north about 9 p.m. b
as late as 11 p.m. in the south. Establishments accustomed to a Briti
clientele may serve dinner earlier. The light Spanish breakfast is a natu
consequence of late dinner. In smaller southern hotels it may not
served at all, which is not a great disadvantage as it will be easily availab
in a local *cafetería*—as late as one likes! Standards of cleanliness are hig
Hot water, however, is not always available and in some areas subj
to drought, water may be cut off for a few hours each day in summ
Showers are more common than baths which are charged extra. So
is not provided. Electric shavers may have to be adapted to a voltage
125 volts.

VOCABULARY

armchair, la butaca (boo-tá-ka)
ashtray, el cenicero (thay-nee-tháy-ro)
bath, el baño (bán-yo)
bathroom, el cuarto de baño (kwár-to day bán-yo)
bed, la cama (ká-ma)
bedroom, la habitación (a-bee-ta-thee-ón), la alcoba (al-kó-
bell, el timbre (tēēm-bray)
bill, la cuenta (kwén-ta)
blanket, la manta (mán-ta)
blind, la persiana (per-see-á-na)
boarding-house, la pensión (pen-see-ón), la casa de huéspe
  (ká-sa day wáys-pay-dhays)
board (full/half), la pensión (completa/media) (kom-pláy-
  máy-dhee-a)
breakfast, el desayuno (day-sa-yōō-no)
chair, la silla (sēél-ya)
chamber-pot, el orinal (o-ree-nál)
clean, limpio (lēēm-pee-o)
coat-hanger, la percha (pér-cha)
cold, frío (frēē-o)
curtain, la cortina (kor-tēē-na)

damp, húmedo (ōō-may-dho)
dining-room, el comedor (ko-may-dhór)
dinner, la cena (tháy-na)
dirty, sucio (sōō-thee-o)
floor, ground (first), el piso bajo (el primer piso) (pēē-so bá-ho /pree-mér pēē-so)
head-waiter, el maître d'hotel (mé-tray do-tél)
heating, la calefacción (ka-lay-fak-thee-ón)
hot, caliente (ka-lee-én-tay)
hotel, el hotel (o-tél)
hot-water bottle, la botella de agua caliente (bo-tél-ya day á-gwa ka-lee-én-tay)
inn, la posada (po-sá-dha)
key, la llave (lyá-vay)
lamp, la lámpara (lám-pa-ra)
lift, el ascensor (as-then-sór)
light, la luz (looth)
lounge, el salón (sa-lón)
lunch, el almuerzo (al-moo-ér-tho)
management, la dirección (dee-rek-thee-ón)
manager, el gerente (hay-rén-tay), el director (dee-rek-tór)
mattress, el colchón (kol-chón)
message, el mensaje (men-sá-hay)
meter, el contador (kon-ta-dhór)
mirror, el espejo (es-páy-ho)
office, la oficina (o-fee-thēē-na)
page-boy, el botones (bo-tó-nays)
pillow, la almohada (al-mo-á-dha)
plug, el enchufe (en-chōō-fay)
porter, el mozo (mó-tho)
proprietor, el dueño (dwén-yo)
receptionist, el (la) recepcionista (ray-thep-thee-on-ēēs-ta)
register, el libro de registro (leé-bro day ray-hēēs-tro)
sheet, la sábana (sá-ba-na)
shower, la ducha (dōō-cha)
shutter, la contraventana (kon-tra-vayn-tá-na)
soap, el jabón (ha-bón)
staircase, la escalera (es-ka-láy-ra)
switch, el interruptor (een-ter-roop-tór)
table (bedside), la mesilla de noche (may-sēēl-ya day nó-chay)
tap, el grifo (grēē-fo)
towel, la toalla (to-ál-ya)
tumbler, el vaso (vá-so)
valet, el criado (kree-á-dho)
wardrobe, el armario (ar-má-ree-o)
washhand basin, el lavabo (la-vá-bo)
window, la ventana (vayn-tá-na)
writing materials, el recado de escribir (ray-ká-do day es-kree-bēēr)

I am Mr. (Mrs., Miss) . . .	Soy el Señor (la Señora, la Señorita) . . .

soy el sayn-yór (la sayn-yó-ra, la sayn-yo-rēē-ta) . . .

I wrote to you reserving a room.	Le escribí para reservar una habitación.

lay es-kree-bēē pá-ra ray-ser-vár ōō-na a-bee-ta-thee-ón

I wrote three weeks ago.	Escribí hace tres semanas.

es-kree-bēē á-thay tres say-má-nas

Did you not get my letter?	¿No recibió usted mi carta?

no ray-thee-bee-ó oos-táydh mee kár-ta

I asked for a second floor room.	Pedí una habitación del segundo piso.

pay-dēē ōō-na a-bee-ta-thee-ón del say-gōōn-do pēē-so

I want a room looking on to the street.	Deseo una habitación que a la calle.

day-sáy-o ōō-na a-bee-ta-thee-ón kay day a la kál-yay

I am looking for a good hotel.	Busco un buen hotel.

bōōs-ko oon boo-én o-tél

Can you give me a room for the night?	¿Puede usted darme una habitación para esta noche?

poo-áy-day oos-táydh dár-may ōō-na a-bee-ta-thee-ón pá-ra és-ta nó-chay

Do you want to see the room?	¿Quiere usted ver la habitación?

kee-áy-ray oos-táydh ver la a-bee-ta-thee-ón

I don't like it.	No me gusta.

no may gōōs-ta

If there is not anything better I shall have to look elsewhere.	Si no hay nada mejor tendré que buscar en otra parte.

see no á-ee ná-dha may-hór ten-dráy kay boos-kár en ó-tra pár-tay

I'll take it.	La tomaré.

la to-ma-ráy

Have my luggage taken up, please.	Sírvase hacer subir mi equipaje.

sēēr-va-say a-thér soo-bēēr mee ay-kee-pá-hay

I am staying for only two or three days.	Me quedo sólo dos o tres días.

may káy-dho só-lo dos o tres dēē-as

I am staying for a week (fortnight) at least.

Me quedo por ocho (quince) días por lo menos.

may káy-dho por ó-cho (kēēn-thay) dēē-as por lo máy-nos

How much do you charge per day with (without) meals?

¿Cuánto cobra usted al día con (sin) las comidas?

kwán-to kó-bra oos-táydh al dēē-a kon (seen) las ko-mēē-dhas

I want a quiet room.

Deseo una habitación tranquila.

day-say-o ōō-na a-bee-ta-thee-ón tran-kēē-la

Is there a lift?

¿Hay ascensor?

á-ee as-then-sór

I cannot sleep; there is too much noise.

No puedo dormir; hay demasiado ruido.

no poo-áy-dho dor-mēēr; á-ee day-ma-see-á-dho roo-ēē-dho

There is no . . . in my room.

No hay . . . en mi habitación.

no á-ee . . . en mee a-bee-ta-thee-ón

The . . . does not work in my room.

El(la) . . . no funciona en mi habitación.

el(la) . . . no foon-thee-ó-na en mee a-bee-ta-thee-ón

The sheets are dirty (damp).

Las sábanas están sucias (húmedas).

las sá-ba-nas es-tán sōō-thee-as (ōō-may-dhas)

The . . . is broken.

El(la) . . . está roto(a).

el(la) . . . es-tá ró-to(a)

Nobody comes when I ring.

Nadie viene cuando llamo.

ná-dee-áy vee-áy-nay kwán-do lyá-mo

I need . . .

Necesito . . .

nay-thay-sēē-to . . .

Bring me . . . !

¡Tráigame . . . !

trá-ee-ga-may . . .

I want to have a bath.

Deseo tomar un baño.

day-sáy-o to-már oon bán-yo

Please open . . .

¡Abra el(la) . . . por favor!

á-bra el(la) por fa-vór

You have not given me . . .

No me ha dado . . .

no may a dá-dho . . .

The light is poor.	No hay bastante luz.
	no á-ee bas-tán-tay looth
The bed is not made.	La cama no está hecha.
	la ká-ma no es-tá áy-cha
I am going to bed at once.	Me acuesto en seguida.
	may a-kwáys-to en say-gēē-dha
Is the tapwater drinkable?	¿Se puede beber el agua del grifo?
	say poo-áy-dhay bay-bér el á-gwa del grēē-fo
At what time do we have lunch (dinner)?	¿A qué hora almorzamos (cenamos)?
	a kay ó-ra al-mor-thá-mos (thay-ná-mos)
I wish to eat earlier.	Deseo comer más temprano.
	day-sáy-o ko-mér mas tem-prá-no
I am expecting a visitor.	Espero una visita.
	es-páy-ro ōō-na vee-sēē-ta
Is there a letter (message) for me?	¿Hay una carta (un mensaje) para mí?
	a-ee ōō-na kár-ta (oon men-sá-hey) pá-ra mee
Did anyone call for me?	¿Vino alguien a buscarme?
	vēē-no ál-gee-en a boos-kár-may
I shall be back at three o'clock.	Estaré de vuelta a las tres.
	es-ta-ráy day voo-él-ta a las tres
Please send him (her) up.	Sírvase decirle que suba.
	sēēr-va-say day-thēēr-lay kay sōō-ba
What is the voltage?	¿Qué es el voltaje?
	kay es el vol-tá-hay
Have these clothes dried.	Haga secar esta ropa.
	á-ga say-kár és-ta ró-pa
Can you sew on this button?	¿Puede usted coser este botón?
	poo-áy-day oos-táydh ko-sér és-tay bo-tón
Can you press my trousers?	¿Puede usted planchar mi pantalón?
	poo-áy-dhay oos-táydh plan-chár mee pan-ta-lón
When does the postman come?	¿A qué hora viene el cartero?
	A kay ó-ra vee-áy-nay el kar-táy-ro

May I use your telephone? ¿Puedo usar su teléfono?
poo-áy-dho oo-sár soo tay-láy-fo-no

Have you a map of the town? ¿Tiene usted un mapa de la ciudad?
tee-áy-nay oos-táydh oon má-pa day la thee-oo-dhádh

Will you get me tickets for ... ? ¿Quiere usted sacarme entradas para ... ?
kee-áy-ray oos-táydh sa-kár-may en-trá-dhas pá-ra ...

Where can I buy ... ? ¿Dónde puedo comprar ... ?
dón-day poo-áy-dho kom-prár ...

I want to post a letter. Deseo echar una carta al correo.
day-sáy-o ay-chár ōō-na kár-ta al ko-ráy-o

Give me key number six, please. Déme la llave número seis por favor.
dáy-may la lyá-vay nōō-may-ro sáy-ees por fa-vór

I'm leaving tomorrow. Me marcho mañana.
may már-cho man-yá-na

I shall have to get up early. Tendré que madrugar.
ten-dráy kay ma-droo-gár

Order me a taxi for ... Mándeme un taxi para las ...
mán-day-may oon táx-ee pá-ra las ...

Please forward my letters to this address. Sírvase remitir mis cartas a esta dirección.
sēēr-va-say ray-mee-tēēr mees kár-tas a és-ta dee-rek-thee-ón

Waken me at... Despiérteme a las ...
des-pee-ér-tay-may a las ...

Knock until I answer. Llame hasta que conteste.
lyá-may á-sta kay kon-tés-tay

Don't disturb me in the morning. No me moleste por la mañana.
no may mo-lés-tay por la man-yá-na

Who is there? ¿Quién está allí?
kee-én es-tá al-yēē

Wait a moment. Espere un momento.
es-páy-ray oon mo-mén-to

Come in!	¡Adelante!
	a-dhay-lán-tay
Make out my bill.	Prepare mi cuenta.
	pray-pá-ray mee kwén-ta
I think there is a mistake.	Creo que se ha equivocado.
	kráy-o kay say a ay-kee-vo-ká-dho
You said the room cost only ...	Usted dijo que la habitación
	costaba solamente ...
	oos-táydh dēē-ho kay la a-bee-ta-thee-ón kos-tá-ba so-la-mén-tay ...
Is the service included?	¿ Está incluido el servicio ?
	es-tá een-kloo-ēē-dho el ser-vēē-thee-o
This is for you.	Esto es para usted.
	és-to es pá-ra oos-táydh
I want a room to change in.	Deseo una habitación para
	cambiarme.
	day-sáy-o ōō-na a-bee-ta-thee-ón pá-ra kám-bee-ár-may
Please bring down my luggage.	Sírvase bajar mi equipaje.
	sēēr-va-say ba-hár mee ay-kee-pá-hay
I have left my ...	He dejado mi ...
	ay day-há-dho mee ...
Will you take a cheque?	¿ Aceptará usted un cheque ?
	a-thayp-ta-rá oos-táydh oon cháy-kay
I shall be in late.	Volveré tarde.
	vol-ver-áy tár-day
Will someone let me in?	¿ Me abrarán ?
	may a-bra-rán
Do you serve English breakfast?	¿ Sirve usted el desayuno
	inglés ?
	sēēr-vay oos-táydh el day-sa-yōō-no een-gláys
Will you give us a packed meal?	¿ Quiere usted darnos una
	merienda empaquetada ?
	kee-áy-ray oos-táydh dár-nos ōō-na may-ree-én-da em-pa-kay-tá-dha
Bring me hot water for shaving.	Tráigame agua caliente para
	afeitarme.
	trá-ee-ga-may á-gwa ka-lee-én-tay pá-ra a-fáy-ee-tár-may

LAUNDRY

For washing list see vocabulary under SHOPPING *pp. 125-7.*

I have some things to be washed.   Tengo algunas cosas para lavar.
 tén-go al-gōō-nas kó-sas pá-ra la-vár

When can I have them back?   ¿Cuándo me las devolverán?
kwán-do me las day-vol-vay-rán

I must have them back by . . .   Importa que las tenga para . . .
eem-pór-ta kay las tén-ga pá-ra . . .

How long will it take?   ¿Cuánto tardará?
kwán-to tar-da-rá

There is a button missing.   Falta un botón.
fál-ta oon bo-tón

I (do not) like my collars   (No) me gustan los cuellos
starched.   almidonados.
(no) may gōōs-tan los koo-áyl-yos al-mee-do-ná-dhos

Can you have a shirt ironed for   ¿Puede usted planchar una
tonight?   camisa para esta noche?
poo-áy-dhay oos-táydh plan-chár ōō-na ka-mēē-sa pá-ra és-ta nó-chay

There are two handkerchiefs   Faltan dos pañuelos.
missing.
fál-tan dos pan-yoo-áy-los

This is not mine.   No es mío.
no es mēē-o

My suit (dress) is stained.   Mi traje está manchado.
mee trá-hay es-tá man-chá-dho

Can you clean it?   ¿Puede limpiarlo?
poo-áy-dhay leem-pee-ár-lo

Press it (them) please.   Plánchemelo por favor.
plán-chay-may-lopor fa-vór

POLICE, PASSPORTS, FORMS

Hotel and boarding-house proprietors are required to fill in a form for the police giving brief details of foreigners' passports and movements. A visa is not necessary for a stay in Spain not exceeding three months. A visa when granted may have to be confirmed after a stated time at the local offices of the *gobierno civil* (go-bee-áyr-no thee-véēl). When obtaining any kind of licence from the authorities it may be necessary to pay in addition to the usual fee a small tax to charity, receipt of which is usually indicated by a special stamp. There are four bodies of police with whom the traveller may come in contact: the *guardia civil* (gwár-dee-a thee-véēl) recognisable by their tricorne hats and green uniform; the *policía armada* who wear a grey uniform and red cap-band. These two corps perform the usual duties of uniformed police, but traffic on the roads is the special care of the *guardia de la circulación* (gwár-dee-a day la theer-koo-la-thee-ón) who wear a blue uniform with white tunic, helmet and baton. There are also plain-clothes police whom the traveller will meet during the examination of passports. At present the Spanish police are empowered to impose fines on the spot in certain cases and to hold charged persons longer without proceedings than would be the case in Britain or other countries.

VOCABULARY

address (permanent), domicilio (fijo) (do-mee-thēē-lee-o fēē-ho)
birth, el nacimiento (na-thee-mee-én-to)
city chambers, el ayuntamiento (a-yoon-ta-mee-én-to)
date, la fecha (fáy-cha)
fine, la multa (mōōl-ta)
first name, nombre (nóm-bray)
foreign money, divisas extranjeras (dee-vēē-sas ex-tran-háy-ras)
form, la ficha (fēē-cha)
married, casado (kas-sá-dho)
passport, el pasaporte (pa-sa-pór-tay)
police, la policía (po-lee-thēē-a)
police station, la comisaría (ko-mee-sa-rēē-a)
purpose of journey, motivo del viaje (mo-tēē-vo del vee-á-hay)
    note: the answer is usually *turismo* (too-rēēs-mo) or business
    negocios (nay-gó-thee-os)
residence (temporary), paradero (pa-ra-dháy-ro)
single, soltero (sol-táy-ro)
surname, apellido (a-payl-yēē-dho)
tax, impuesto (eem-pwáys-to)
valid until, válido hasta (vá-lee-dho á-sta)
visa, el visado (vee-sá-dho)
work permit, el permiso de trabajo (per-mēē-so day tra-bá-ho)

| May I have your passport? | ¿Puede darme su pasaporte? |
| | poo-áy-dhay dár-may soo pa-sa-pór-tay |

| I intend to stay . . . days. | Pienso quedarme . . . días. |
| | pee-én-so kay-dhár-may . . . dēē-as |

| Are you a foreigner? | ¿Es usted extranjero? |
| | es oos-táydh ex-tran-háy-ro |

| I am a British (American) subject. | Soy súbdito británico (ameri-cano). |
| | soy sōōb-dee-to bree-tá-nee-ko (a-may-ree-ká-no) |

| Please come with me. | Venga conmigo por favor. |
| | vén-ga kon-mēē-go por fa-vór |

| Please fill up this form. | Haga el favor de completar esta ficha. |
| | á-ga el fa-vór day kom-play-tár és-ta fēē-cha |

| Where have you come from? | ¿De dónde llega usted? |
| | day dón-day lyáy-ga oos-táydh |

| Where are you going? | ¿A dónde va usted? |
| | a dón-day va oos-táydh |

| I'll give it back to you . . . | Se lo devolveré . . . |
| | say lo day-vol-vay-ráy |

| I must detain you. | Debo detenerle. |
| | dáy-bo day-ten-ér-lay |

| For what reason? | ¿Con qúe motivo? |
| | kon kay mo-tēē-vo |

| I wish to inform the Consul. | Deseo informar al consulado. |
| | day-sáy-o een-for-már al kon-soo-lá-dho |

| I wish to consult a lawyer. | Deseo consultar con un abogado. |
| | day-sáy-o kon-sōōl-tar kon oon a-bo-gá-dho |

| I have been robbed. | Me han robado. |
| | may an ro-bá-dho |

| Can you describe it? | ¿Puede usted describirlo? |
| | poo-áy-dhay oos-táydh des-kree-bēēr-lo |

| What was in the wallet? | ¿Qué contenía la cartera? |
| | kay kon-tayn-ēē-a la kar-táy-ra |

What was this man like?	**¿Cómo era este hombre?**
	kó-mo áy-ra és-tay óm-bray
Is that the thief?	**¿Es éste el ladrón?**
	es és-tay el la-drón
I have lost . . .	**He perdido . . .**
	ay per-dēē-dho

VILLAS

There are now many agencies in this country through which one may rent a Spanish villa in summer, obtaining at the same time the services of a maid. Rather than ask the latter to give an account of her shopping for you (such an account being liable to fluctuations due to changes in the price and quality of produce), take an occasional stroll through the market with an eye to these factors and you are unlikely to suffer any gross deception. It is well to be clear about what household goods you expect to find and the extent of your liability for damage or theft. Ascertain whether there is any possibility of water being cut off.

VOCABULARY

armchair, el sillón de brazos (seel-yón day brá-thos)
basket, el cesto (thés-to), la cesta (thés-ta)
bathroom, el cuarto de baño (kwár-to day bán-yo)
bed, la cama (ká-ma)
bedroom, la alcoba (al-kó-ba)
blanket, la manta (mán-ta)
blind, la persiana (per-see-á-na)
blocked, obturado (ob-too-rá-dho)
brazier, el brasero (bra-sáy-ro)
broken, roto (ró-to)
broom, la escoba (es-kó-ba)
bucket, el cubo (kōō-bo)
bulb, la bombilla (bom-bēēl-ya)
chair, la silla (sēēl-ya)
clean, limpio (lēēm-pee-o)
crockery, la loza (ló-tha)
cup, la taza (tá-tha)
detergent, el detergente (day-ter-hén-tay)
dining-room, el comedor (ko-may-dhór)
dinner, la cena (tháy-na)
dirty, sucio (sōō-thee-o)
dish, el plato (plá-to)
dishes, la vajilla (va-hēēl-ya)
drain, el desagüe (day-ság-way)
dustman, el basurero (ba-soo-ráy-ro)
electricity, la electricidad (ay-lek-tree-thee-dádh)

fibre (for washing-up), el estropajo (es-tro-pá-ho)
floor, el suelo (swáy-lo)
food, la comida (ko-mēē-dha)
fork, el tenedor (te-ne-dhór)
frying-pan, la sartén (sar-tén)
glass, el vaso (vá-so)
guest, el huésped (wáys-pedh), el invitado (een-vee-tá-dho)
iron, la plancha (plán-cha)
jug, el jarro (há-ro)
key, la llave (lyá-vay)
knife, el cuchillo (koo-chēēl-yo)
lamp, la lámpara (lám-pa-ra)
landing, el descanso de la escalera (des-kán-so day la es-ka-láy-ra)
landlord (lady), el dueño (dueña) (dwáyn-yo, -ya)
light, la luz (looth)
lunch, el almuerzo (al-moo-ér-tho)
maid, la criada (kree-á-dha)
market, el mercado (mer-ká-dho)
mattress, el colchón (kol-chón)
meal, la comida (ko-mēē-dha)
meter, el contador (kon-ta-dhór)
oven, el horno (ór-no)
pillow, la almohada (al-mo-á-dha)
pipe, el tubo (tōō-bo)
place (at table), el cubierto (koo-bee-ér-to)
plug (electric), el enchufe (en-chōō-fay)
plug (of basin), el tapón (ta-pón)
plumber, el plomero (plo-máy-ro)
power-cut, el apagón (a-pa-gón)
refrigerator, la nevera (nay-váy-ra)
rent, el alquiler (al-kee-lér)
rubbish, la basura (ba-sōō-ra)
saucepan, la cacerola (ka-thay-ró-la)
sheet, la sábana (sá-ba-na)
shopping, las compras (kóm-pras)
shopping-basket, la cesta (tháys-ta)
shower, la ducha (dōō-cha)
shutter, la contraventana (kon-tra-vayn-tá-na)
sink, el fregadero (fray-ga-dháy-ro)
sitting-room, la sala de estar (sá-la day es-tár)
soap, el jabón (ha-bón)
spoon, la cuchara (koo-chá-ra)
stairs, la escalera (ays-ka-láy-ra)
stewpot, la olla (ól-ya)
sun-roof, la terraza (tay-rá-tha), la azotea (a-tho-táy-a)
switch, el interruptor (een-ter-roop-tór)
table, la mesa (máy-sa)
tap, el grifo (grēē-fo)
tea, el té (tay)

teaspoon, la cucharita (koo-cha-rēē-ta)
tea-pot, la tetera (tay-táy-ra)
tin-opener, el abrelatas (a-bray-lá-tas)
toilet, el wáter (vá-ter)
towel, la toalla (to-ál-ya)
washhand basin, el lavabo (la-vá-bo)
waste-paper basket, el cesto para papeles (tháys-to pá-pa-páy-lays)
window, la ventana (vayn-tá-na)
yard, el patio (pá-tee-o)

I am looking for rooms to rent. Estoy buscando habitacion«
                                        para alquilar.
es-tóy boos-kán-do a-bee-ta-thee-ón-ays pá-ra al-keel-ár

How much is the rent?   ¿Cuánto es el alquiler?
                    kwán-to es el al-keel-ér

What is included in the price?   ¿Qué va incluido con el preci«
            kay va een-kloo-ēē-dho kon el práy-thee-o

What furniture is there?   ¿Qué muebles hay?
                        kay moo-áy-blays á-ee

Write down the conditions, Apunte las condiciones, p«
please.   favor.
        a-pōōn-tay las kon-dee thee-ó-nays por fa-vór

I want a daily maid.   Quiero una sirvienta cada dí
        kee-áy-ro ōō-na seer-vee-én-ta ká-dha dēē-a

How much an hour does she get? ¿Cuánto recibe por hora?
                kwán-to ray-thēē-bay por ó-ra

How much do you ask?   ¿Cuánto pide usted?
                kwán-to pēē-dhay oos-táydh

. . . per hour (day, week).   . . . por hora (al día, p«
                                          semana).
        . . . por ó-ra, (al dēē-a, por say-má-na)

What is your name, miss?   ¿Cómo se llama usted,
                                          señorita?
        kó-mo say lyá-ma oos-táydh sayn-yo-rēē-ta

Do the shopping.   Haga las compras.
                    á-ga las kóm-pras

Tell me what you spend.   Dígame lo que gaste.
dēē-ga-may lo kay gás-tay

Is this enough?   ¿ Es bastante?
es bas-tán-tay

Bring me the change.   Tráigame el cambio.
trá-ee-ga-may el kám-bee-o

Make the beds.   Haga las camas.
á-ga las ká-mas

Sweep the rooms.   Barra las habitaciones.
bár-ra las a-bee-ta-thee-ó-nays

Will you prepare the meals? ¿ Quiere usted preparar las
         comidas?
kee-áy-ray oos-táydh pray-pa-rár las ko-mēē-dhas

Wash and iron these clothes. Lave y planche esta ropa.
lá-vay ee plán-chay és-ta ró-pa

Clean this.   Limpie esto.
lēēm-pee-ay és-to

Will you wash up?   ¿ Quiere usted fregar?
kee-áy-ray oos-táydh fray-gár

The water must be boiling. El agua tiene que estar hirvi-
         endo.
el á-gwa tee-áy-nay kay es-tár eer-vee-én-do

At what time can you come? ¿ A qué hora puede usted
         venir?
a kay ó-ra poo-áy-dhay oos-táydh vay-nēēr

Can you stay and baby sit? ¿ Puede quedarse y cuidar al
         niño?
poo-áy-dhay kay-dár-say ee kwee-dhár al nēēn-yo

We are going out tonight. Vamos a salir esta noche.
vá-mos a sa-lēēr és-ta nó-chay

How many hours did you work ¿ Cuántas horas trabajó hoy?
today?
kwán-tas ó-ras tra-ba-hó oy

We shall have a guest tonight. Tendremos un invitado esta
         noche.
ten-dráy-mos oon een-vee-tá-dho és-ta nó-chay

Lay four places at table.   Ponga cuatro cubiertos.
pón-ga kwá-tro koo-bee-ér-tos

Cook us a local dish.   Háganos un plato típico.
á-ga-nos oon plá-to tēē-pee-ko

The meal was excellent.   La comida era excelente.
la ko-mēē-dha áy-ra ex-thay-lén-tay

Fetch a plumber immediately.   Busque un plomero en seguida
bōōs-kay oon plo-máy-ro en say-gēē-dha

Give the dustman this tip.   Dé esta propina al basurero.
day és-ta pro-pēē-na al ba-soo-ráy-ro

You have looked after us very   Usted nos ha cuidado mu
well.   bien.
oos-táydh nos a kwee-dá-dho mwee bee-én

SIGHTSEEING AND SEASIDE

There are many guide books which provide information about places
interest in Spanish towns and the excursions which may be made from then
and only a few suggestions are given here. A local map may be obtaine
from a bookstall or the local tourist information office. The word *muse*
(moo-sáy-o) means both a museum and an art gallery. On certain day
as an inducement to the local population the entry fee is reduced. On
should not go round a church if mass is being said at the high altar, an
women are expected to cover their heads and arms. Resist gypsy blandis
ments with regard to displays of flamenco as the best troupes have in ar
case arrangements with the local tourist agencies or hotels. If you acce
the services in a *bodega* (bo-dháy-ga) tavern, of a guitarist or singer, d
not assume that they will perform for you for hours on end just for th
love of the thing or a small tip. As a tourist you will be regarded by th
beggars as a soft target; it is up to yourself whether you choose to sa
once *Perdone hermano* (per-dó-nay er-má-no), "Sorry, brother!" and there
after ignore any importuning, or get rid of some small change and elicit
Dios se lo pague (dee-ós say lo pá-gay), "God reward you".

MADRID	Museo del Prado, main boulevards, Puerta del So the Retiro park, Royal Palace, Plaza Mayo Excursions to Toledo, the Escorial.
BARCELONA	Main boulevards, the Barrio Gótico (old quarter the Pueblo Español (exhibition of region products, etc.). Excursions to Montserra Tarragona.
SANTANDER	Excursions to Altamira (prehistoric paintings).
TOLEDO	Cathedral, churches, synagogue; the Alcázar.

RDOBA	Cathedral.
VILLA	Cathedral and Giralda; the Alcázar.
RANADA	The Alhambra palace; the Sacromonte.
NTIAGO DE COMPOSTELA	Cathedral façade and square.

VOCABULARY

altar-piece, el retablo (ray-táb-lo)
Arab, (el) árabe (á-ra-bay)
avenue, la avenida (a-vay-nēē-dha)
baroque, barroco (ba-ró-ko)
battlements, las almenas (al-máy-nas)
bishop, el obispo (o-bēēs-po)
bridge, el puente (pwén-tay)
building, el edificio (ay-dhee-fēē-thee-o)
buried, enterrado (en-ter-á-dho)
castle, el castillo (kas-tēēl-yo)
catalogue, el catálogo (ka-tá-lo-go)
cathedral, la catedral (ka-tay-drál)
century, el siglo (sēē-glo)
chapel, la capilla (ka-pēēl-ya)
church, la iglesia (ee-gláy-see-a)
Cid, el, Medieval Spanish hero (theed)
Colón, Columbus (ko-lón)
excursion, la excursión (ex-koor-see-ón)
façade, la fachada (fa-chá-dha)
fortress, el alcázar (al-ká-thar)
gate, ornamental, la reja (ráy-ha)
gipsy, el gitano (hee-tá-no)
Goth, el godo (gó-dho)
guide, guide-book, el guía (gēē-a), la guía (gēē-a)
king, el rey (ráy-ee)
lake, el lago (lá-go)
lake, ornamental, el estanque (es-tán-kay)
library, la biblioteca (beeb-lee-o-táy-ka)
map, el mapa (má-pa)
miracle, el milagro (mee-lá-gro)
Moor, el moro (mó-ro)
Moorish, morisco (mo-rēēs-ko)
mosque, la mezquita (meth-kēē-ta)
mountain, el monte (món-tay), la montaña (mon-tán-ya)
mozárabe, Christian under Moorish rule (moth-á-ra-bay)
outskirts, las afueras (a-fwáy-ras)
painting, la pintura (peen-tōō-ra), el cuadro (kwá-dro), el lienzo (lee-én-tho)
palace, el palacio (pa-lá-thee-o)
park, el parque (pár-kay)
Parliament, las Cortes (kór-tays)
pilgrimage, la romería (ro-may-rēē-a)

portrait, el retrato (ray-trá-to)
postcard, la tarjeta postal (tar-háy-ta pos-tál)
post office, Correos (ko-ráy-os)
queen, la reina (ráy-ee-na)
relic, la reliquia (ray-lēē-kee-a)
Reyes Católicos, Ferdinand & Isabella, 15th c. (ráy-ay
    ka-tó-lee-kos)
sculpture, la escultura (es-kool-tōō-ra)
sexton, el sacristán (sa-krees-tán)
square, la plaza (plá-tha)
stained-glass window, la vidriera (veed-ree-áy-ra)
street, la calle (kál-yay)
tomb, la tumba (tōōm-ba)
tower, la torre (tó-ray)
town, la ciudad (thee-oo-dádh)
town hall, el ayuntamiento (a-yoon-ta-mee-én-to)
university, la universidad (oo-nee-ver-see-dádh)

Is this the right way to . . . ?　　¿Vamos bien para . . . ?
　　　　　　　　　　　　vá-mos bee-én pá-ra . . .

Would you be so kind as to　¿Tendría usted la bondad d
　direct me to . . . ?　　　　decirme dónde está . . .
　ten-drēē-a oos-táydh la bon-dádh day day-thēēr-may dón-day es-tá . . .

Cross the road.　　　　　　Cruce la calle.
　　　　　　　　　　krōō-thay la kál-yay

On the opposite pavement.　En la acera de enfrente.
　　　　　　　　　en la a-tháy-ra day en-frén-tay

On the other side of the square.　Al otro lado de la plaza.
　　　　　　　　　al ót-ro lá-dho day la plá-tha

The first (opening) on the left　La primera (bocacalle) a l
　(right).　　　　　　　　izquierda (derecha).
　la pree-máy-ra (bo-ka-kál-yay) a la eeth-kee-áyr-da (day-ráy-cha)

Go straight on.　　　　　　Siga todo derecho.
　　　　　　　　　sēē-ga tó-dho day-ráy-cho

Turn right (left).　　　　　Tome por la derecha (izquierda
　　　　　　　tó-may por la day-ráy-cha (eeth-kee-áyr-da)

This way. That way.　　　　Por aquí. Por allá.
　　　　　　　　por a-kēē. por al-yá

Have you a map of the town?　¿Tiene usted un mapa de l
　　　　　　　　　　　　ciudad?
　tee-áy-nay oos-táydh oon má-pa day la thee-oo-dhádh

want to visit the old quarter.   Deseo visitar el barrio viejo.
day-sáy-o vee-see-tár el bá-ree-o vee-áy-ho

s there a bus?   ¿Hay un autobús?
á-ee oon ow-to-bōōs

Vhere is the bus stop?   ¿Dónde está la parada?
dón-day es-tá la pa-rá-dha

s this the terminus?   ¿Es el fin del trayecto?
es el feen del tra-yék-to

Iave you a list of excursions? ¿Tiene usted una lista de
excursiones?
tee-áy-nay oos-táydh ōō-na lēēs-ta day ex-koor-see-ó-nays

Ve want to go on a tour to ...   Deseamos hacer una excursión
a ...
dey-say-á-mos a-thér ōō-na ex-koor-see-ón a ...

Ve want to be together.   Deseamos estar juntos.
day-say-á-mos es-tár hōōn-tos

s there a guide who speaks ¿Hay un guía que hable
English?   inglés?
á-ee oon gēē-a kay á-blay een-gláys

Vould those who speak English Por favor, vengan conmigo los
(French) come with me.   de lengua inglesa (francesa).
por fa-vór ven-gán kon-mēē-go los day lén-gwa een-gláy-sa (fran-tháy-sa)

Iow much is the tour?   ¿Qué es el precio de la
excursión?
kay es el práy-thee-o day la ex-koor-see-ón

Po we have to pay the guide?   ¿Tenemos que pagar al guía?
te-náy-mos kay pa-gár al gēē-a

am looking for ...   Busco ...
bōōs-ko

am lost.   Estoy perdido.
es-tóy per-dēē-dho

an one go on foot?   ¿Se puede ir a pie?
say poo-áy-dhay eer a pee-áy

it far?   ¿Está lejos?
es-tá láy-hos

What is that building? ¿Qué es ese edificio?
kay es é-say ay-dhee-fēē-thee-o

Where can I get entrance tickets? ¿Dónde se sacan las entradas?
dón-day say sá-kan las en-trá-dhas

Is it open? ¿Está abierto?
es-tá a-bee-ér-to

When will it open? ¿A qué hora se abre?
a kay ó-ra say á-bray

When does it close? ¿A qué hora se cierra?
a kay ó-ra say thee-áy-ra

Can we go in? ¿Se puede entrar?
say poo-áy-dhay en-trár

We wish to see . . . Deseamos ver . . .
day-say-á-mos ver . . .

Can we take photographs? ¿Se puede sacar fotos?
say poo-áy-dhay sa-kár fó-tos

Follow the guide. Siga al guía.
sēē-ga al gēē-a

Have you postcards showing ¿Tiene usted tarjetas postales
the work of . . . ? de la obra de . . . ?
tee-áy-nay oos-táydh tar-háy-tas pos-tá-lays day la ó-bra day . . .

Painters of the Spanish school. Pintores de la escuela española.
peen-tó-rays day la es-kwáy-la es-pan-yó-la

. . . dates from the fifteenth . . . es del siglo quince.
century.
. . . es del sēē-glo kēēn-thay

. . . was built by . . . . . . fué construido por . . .
fway kon-stroo-ēē-dho por . . .

I haven't much time. No tengo mucho tiempo.
no tén-go mōō-cho tee-ém-po

How long does it take? ¿Cuánto se tarda?
kwán-to say tár-da

Let us sit down for a while. Sentémonos un rato.
sen-táy-mo-nos oon rá-to

Can we go round alone? ¿Podemos ir solos?
po-dháy-mos eer só-los

When does the next tour start? ¿Cuándo empieza la próxima excursión (visita)?

kwán-do em-pee-áy-tha la próx-ee-ma ex-koor-see-ón (vee-sēē-ta)

It is magnificent (charming). Es magnífico (encantador).

es mag-nēē-fee-ko (en-kan-ta-dhór)

I am too tired to go farther. Estoy demasiado cansado para ir más lejos.

es-tóy day-ma-see-á-dho kan-sá-dho pá-ra eer mas láy-hos

I have seen enough for today. He visto bastante para hoy.

ay vēēs-to bas-tán-tay pá-ra oy

Where can we shelter? ¿Dónde podemos guarecernos?

dón-day po-dháy-mos gwa-ray-thér-nos

Free entry. Entrada gratuita.

en-trá-dha gra-twēē-ta

Of what period is it? ¿De qué época es?

day kay áy-po-ka es

Who built it? ¿Quién lo construyó?

kee-én lo kon-stroo-yó

It is open (closed). Está abierto (cerrado).

es-tá a-bee-ér-to (thay-rá-dho)

Come back tomorrow. Vuelva mañana.

voo-áyl-va man-yá-na

AT THE BEACH

Restrictions on beachwear are less severe than formerly, but it must still
be confined to the beach. In many places it is necessary to change in a
bathing-hut, where one's clothes may be left on a coat-hanger under some
sort of supervision although their safety is not guaranteed.

VOCABULARY

air mattress, el colchón de aire (kol-chón day á-ee-ray)
back stroke, la braza de espalda (brá-tha day es-pál-da)
ball, la pelota (pay-ló-ta)
basketball, el baloncesto (ba-lon-tháys-to)
bathing cap, el gorro de baño (gó-ro day bán-yo)
bathing costume, el traje de baño (trá-hay day bán-yo)
bathing costume (two piece), el traje de baño (de dos piezas)
(trá-hay day bán-yo day dos pee-áy-thas)

bathing hut, la caseta de baño (ka-sáy-ta day bán-yo)
bay, la bahía (ba-ēē-a)
beach, la playa (plá-ya)
beach bag, la bolsa de playa (ból-sa day plá-ya)
bikini, el bikini (bee-kēē-nee)
boat, la canoa (ka-nó-a), el bote (bó-tay)
bucket, el cubo (kōō-bo)
buoy, la boya (bó-ya)
canoe, la canoa (ka-nó-a)
chair, folding, la silla plegable (sēēl-ya play-gá-blay)
cliff, el acantilado (a-kan-tee-lá-dho)
clothes, la ropa (ró-pa)
coast, la costa (kós-ta)
crab, el cangrejo (kan-gráy-ho)
cramp, el entumecimiento (en-too-may-thee-mee-én-to)
current, el corriente (ko-ree-én-tay)
dive, to, saltar (sal-tár), zambullirse (tham-bool-yēēr-say)
diving board, la plataforma (pla-ta-fór-ma)
dress, to, vestirse (ves-tēēr-say)
drown, to, ahogarse (a-o-gár-say)
dune, la duna (dōō-na)
fish, el pez (peth)
fish, to, pescar (pes-kár)
flippers, las aletas para nadar (a-láy-tas pá-ra na-dhár)
goggles, las gafas de inmersión (gá-fas day een-mer-see-ón)
harpoon, el arpón (ar-pón)
jelly-fish, la medusa (may-dhōō-sa)
lighthouse, el faro (fá-ro)
motorboat, el deslizador (des-leeth-a-dhór)
oars, los remos (ráy-mos)
outboard motor, el fuera bordo (foo-áy-ra bór-do)
raft, la balsa (bál-sa)
reef, el escollo (es-kól-yo)
rock, la roca (ró-ka), la peña (páyn-ya)
row, to, remar (ray-már)
sail, to, dar un paseo en bote (dar oon pa-sáy-o en bó-tay)
sails, las velas (váy-las)
sand, la arena (a-ráy-na)
sandals, las alpargatas (al-par-gá-tas)
sea, el mar (mar)
shade, la sombra (sóm-bra)
shark, el tiburón (tee-boo-rón)
shell, la concha (kón-cha)
shingle, los guijarros (gee-há-ros)
shiver, to, tiritar (tee-ree-tár)
shower, la ducha (dōō-cha)
spade, la pala (pá-la)
spring-board, el trampolín (tram-po-lēēn)
sun, el sol (sol)
sunbathe, tomar un baño de sol (to-mar oon bán-yo day sol

sunglasses, las gafas de sol (gá-fas day sol)
sunshade, el quitasol (kee-ta-sól)
sunstroke, la insolación (een-so-la-thee-ón)
sun-tan lotion, la loción para broncear (lo-thee-ón pá-ra bron-thay-ár)
surf, el olaje (o-lá-hay)
surf board, la plancha de deslizamiento (plán-cha day des-leeth-a-mee-én-to)
surf riding, el patinaje sobre las olas (pa-tee-ná-hay so-bray las ó-las)
swimming, la natación (na-ta-thee-ón)
swimming pool, la piscina (pees-thēē-na)
tan, el bronceado (bron-thay-á-dho)
tandem, la bicicleta acuática (bee-thee-cláy-ta a-kwá-tee-ka)
tide (high/low), la marea alta/baja (ma-ráy-a ál-ta/bá-ha)
towel, la toalla (to-ál-ya)
undress, to, desnudarse (des-noo-dhár-say)
water, el agua (á-gwa)
water-skiing, el esquí acuático (es-kēē a-kwá-tee-ko)
wave, la ola (ó-la)
whirlpool, el remolino de agua (ray-mo-lēē-no day á-gwa)

Which is the way to the beach? ¿ Por dónde se va a la playa?
por dón-day say va a la plá-ya

Is it far? ¿ Está lejos?
es-tá láy-hos

Is there a bus? ¿ Hay un autobús?
á-ee oon ow-to-bōōs

Where can we bathe? ¿ Dónde podemos bañarnos?
dón-day po-dháy-mos ban-yár-nos

Where does one change? ¿ Dónde hay que cambiarse?
dón-day á-ee kay kam-bee-ár-say

Do you have a coat-hanger? ¿ Tiene usted una percha?
tee-áy-nay oos-taydh ōō-na pér-cha

What is the number? ¿ Qué es el número?
kay es el nōō-may-ro

I want to hire ... Deseo alquilar ...
day-sáy-o al-kee-lár ...

A rowing boat (sailing boat, outboard motorboat). Un bote de remos (de vela, de fuera bordo).
oon bó-tay day ráy-mos (day váy-la, day foo-áy-ra bór-do)

What is the water like?   ¿Cómo está el agua?
kó-mo es-tá el á-gwa

Marvellous!   ¡Estupenda!
es-too-pén-da

Is it deep?   ¿Está honda?
es-tá ón-da

I cannot swim very well.   No sé nadar muy bien.
no say na-dhár mwee bee-én

Be careful, there is a strong current.   Cuidado, hay un corriente fuerte.
kwee-dhá-dho á-ee oon ko-ree-én-tay foo-áyr-tay

Watch out for jelly-fish.   Cuidado con las medusas.
kwee-dhá-dho kon las may-dhōō-sas

The water is warm (cold).   El agua está caliente (fría).
el á-gwa es-tá ka-lee-én-tay (frēē-a)

I only want to sunbathe.   No quiero más que tomar un baño de sol.
no kee-áy-ro mas kay to-már oon bán-yo day sol

You will get sunstroke.   Tendrá una insolación.
ten-drá ōō-na een-so-la-thee-ón

How tanned (pale) you are!   ¡Qué bronceado(a) (pálido/a) está usted!
kay bron-thay-á dho (a) (pá-lee-dho/a) es-tá oos-táydh

Is it safe to swim here?   ¿Se puede bañarse aquí con seguridad?
say poo-áy-dhay ban-yár-say a-kēē kon say-goo-ree-dádh

Are our things safe here?   ¿Están seguras nuestras cosas aquí?
es-tán say-gōō-ras noo-áys-tras kó-sas a-kēē

SPORTS, GAMES AND ENTERTAINMENT

FOOTBALL

This is the favourite sport of most Spaniards and one at which they excel. The following words and phrases may even enable the enthusiast to get the gist of any reported match in a newspaper. Most matches take place on Sunday afternoons. Only a little rugby football is played, mainly in the north.

VOCABULARY

back, el defensa (day-fén-sa)
ball, el balón (ba-lón), la pelota (pay-ló-ta)
centre forward, el delantero centro (day-lan-táy-ro thén-tro)
centre half, el medio centro (máy-dhee-o thén-tro)
championship, el campeonato (kam-pay-on-á-to)
clearance, el despeje (des-páy-hay)
corner, la esquina (es-kēē-na)
corner-kick, el saque de esquina (sá-kay day es-kēē-na)
cross-bar, el larguero (lar-gáy-ro)
draw, el empate (em-pá-tay)
fan, el aficionado (a-fee-thee-o-ná-dho)
football (game), el fútbol (fōōt-bol)
forward, el delantero (day-lan-táy-ro)
foul, la falta (fál-ta)
free-kick, el golpe franco (gól-pay frán-ko), el saque libre (sá-kay lēē-bray)
goal (score), el gol (gol), el tanto (tán-to)
goal (place), la meta (máy-ta), el portal (por-tál), la portería (por-tay-rēē-a), el marco (már-ko), la puerta (poo-áyr-ta)
goal-keeper, el portero (por-táy-ro), el guardametas (gwar-da-máy-tas)
half, first, (second), el primer (segundo) tiempo (pree-mér /say-gōōn-do tee-ém-po)
half back, el medio (máy-dhee-o)
half-time, el descanso (des-kán-so)
header, el remate de cabeza (ray-má-tay day ka-báy-tha), el cabezazo (ka-bay-thá-tho)
inside, interior (een-tay-ree-ór)
kick, la patada (pa-tá-dha)
left, izquierdo(a) (eeth-kee-ér-do/a)
linesman, el juez de banda (línea) (hoo-éth day bán-da /lēē-nay-a), el linier (lee-nee-ér)
line-up, la alineación (a-lee-nay-a-thee-ón)
match, el partido (par-tēē-dho)

off-side, fuera de juego (foo-áy-ra day hoo-áy-go)
pass, el pase (pá-say)
penalty, el penalty (pén-al-tay)
penalty area, el área de castigo (á-ray-a day kas-tēē-go)
player, el jugador (hoo-ga-dhór), el futbolista (foot-bol-ēēs-ta)
referee, el árbitro (ár-bee-tro)
right, derecho(a) (day-ráy-cho/a)
score, la marca (már-ka), el tanto (tán-to)
season, la temporada (tem-po-rá-dha)
shot, el tiro (tēē-ro), el disparo (dees-pá-ro)
stadium, el estadio (es-tá-dhee-o)
stand, la tribuna (tree-bōō-na)
tackle, la entrada (en-trá-dha)
team, el equipo (ay-kēē-po)
terracing, las gradas (grá-dhas)
throw-in, el saque de banda (sá-kay day bán-da)
title-holders, el equipo titular (ay-kēē-po tee-too-lár)
touch-line, la línea de banda (lēē-nay-a day bán-da)
trainer, el entrenador (en-tren-a-dhór)
whistle, el pito (pēē-to)
win, ganar (ga-nár)
wing, el extremo (ex-tráy-mo)

They drew two all.	Han empatado a dos tanto.
	an em-pa-tá-dho a dos tán-to
They won (lost) three one.	Ganaron (perdieron) por tres a uno.
	ga-ná-ron (per-dee-áy-ron) por tres a ōō-no
To score a goal.	Marcar (conseguir) un gol.
	mar-kár (con-say-gēēr) oon gol
Scored by X from a pass by Y.	Marcado por X a pase de Y
	mar-ká-dho por . . . a pá-say day . . .
One all.	Empate a uno.
	em-pá-tay a ōō-no
Sent off.	Expulsado.
	expool-sá-dho
Four all.	Cuatro tantos.
	kwá-tro tán-tos

BULLFIGHTING

This rather cruel sport is still quite popular in Spain, especially with
tourists. Bullfights are held on Sundays and on feast days and sometimes
mid-week, in the late afternoon. The most important are to be found in
Madrid, Seville and other towns during their fairs. Generally three bull-
fighters appear with their respective teams and kill two bulls each. They
occupy a position in a league table according to points scored. The number
of points depends on whether they win an ear, tail, hoof, applause, circuit
of the ring, etc. As the tiered seats are of stone one should hire a cushion.
As might be expected the seats nearest the ring are dearest, the *contrabarrera*
(kon-tra-ba-ráy-ra) and those farthest away are cheapest, the *tendido alto*
(ten-dēē-dho ál-to). Medium-priced seats between these are called the
tendido. The rows of seats are numbered from the front and each section
of *tendido* between aisles is given a letter of the alphabet. Seats in the
shade *sombra* (sóm-bra) are dearer than those in the sun *sol* (sol). The
bull is played with capes, has darts placed in its shoulders and is angered
and weakened with a lance. The bullfighter then plays it with a small
cape as close as he dares and finally kills it with a sword.

GLOSSARY OF TERMS

el aficionado (a-fee-thee-o-ná-dho) =fan
la almohadilla (al-mo-adh-ēēl-ya) =cushion
el arrastre (a-rás-tray) =dragging out of the carcass by mules
el aviso (a-vēē-so) =warning from the president's box
las banderillas (ban-day-rēēl-yas) =pairs of beribboned darts
el banderillero (ban-day-reel-yáy-ro) =man who places the darts
bravo (brá-vo) =fierce
el brindis (brēēn-dees) =dedication of the bull to someone
el burladero (boor-la-dháy-ro) =wooden refuge
el callejón (kal-yáy-hón) =alley round the ring
la capa (ká-pa) =cape
la corrida (ko-rēē-dha) =bullfight
la cogida (ko-hēē-dha) =toss
la cuadrilla (kwa-drēēl-ya) =bullfighting team
derecho (day-ráy-cho) =a pass with the right arm
el descabello (des-ka-bél-yo) =coup de grâce given with a dagger or special
    sword
el diestro (dee-és-tro) =bullfighter
embestir(i) (em-bes-tēēr) =to charge
la entera (en-táy-ra) =sword-stroke to the hilt
la espada (es-pá-dha) =sword
el espada (es-pá-dha) =bullfighter
el espontáneo (es-pon-tá-nay-o) =member of public who decides to
    participate
la estocada (es-to-ká-dha) =sword-thrust made with...
el estoque (es-tó-kay) =bullfighter's sword

estropear (es-tro-pay-ár) =to spoil the bull (often said of the picadores)
la faena (fa-áy-na) =job, task
el farol (fa-ról) =a whirling pass of the cape
el ganado (ga-ná-dho) =livestock: the bulls
hombros, en (en óm-bros) =shoulder high
la manoletina (ma-no-lay-tēē-na) =pass with the cape held from behind the back
manso (mán-so) =tame
el matador (ma-ta-dhór) =bullfighter
el momento de la verdad (mo-mén-to day la ver-dádh) =the kill
el mozo de capa (mó-tho day ká-pa) =assistant bullfighter
la muleta (moo-láy-ta) =small cape on a stick
el natural (na-too-rál) =a common pass
el novillo (no-vēēl-yo) =young bull
el novillero (no-veel-yáy-ro) =apprentice bullfighter
la novillada (no-veel-yá-dha) =bullfight with young bulls
la oreja (o-ráy-ha) =ear
el pase (pá-say) =pass with a cape
el paseo (pa-sáy-o) =preliminary parade
la pata (pá-ta) =hoof
pecho, de (day páy-cho) =pass across the chest
el peso (páy-so) =weight of bull, chalked above the *toril*
el picador (pee-ka-dhór) =mounted man with lance
el pinchazo (peen-chá-tho) =incomplete sword-thrust
pitos (pēē-tos) =whistles of disapproval
la plaza (plá-tha) =the bullring
el quite (kēē-tay) =diverting of the bull's attention
el rabo (rá-bo) =tail
el redondel (ray-dhón-del) =bullring
el rejoneador (ray-hon-ay-a-dhór) =mounted man who places darts
la res (res) =the bull
rodillas, de (day rodh-ēēl-yas) =kneeling
el ruedo (roo-áy-dho) =the ring
la suerte (soo-áyr-tay) =stage of bullfight
el tercio (tér-thee-o) = ditto
el torero (to-ráy-ro) =bullfighter
el toril (to-rēēl) =bull-pen
el toro de lidia (tó-ro day lēē-dhee-a) =fighting bull
la vara (vá-ra) =lance
la varonica (va-ró-nee-ka) =a pass in which the body revolves contrariwise to the bull's charge.
la vuelta (voo-áyl-ta) =lap of the ring

OTHER SPORTS, GAMES AND ENTERTAINMENT

Spain has other sports to offer: fishing, golf, horse-racing, show jumping, ski-ing, swimming (see *At the Beach*) and pelota which is to be found in the

Basque country and is a ball game played against a wall by two players
and which demands agility and stamina. With regard to indoor pastimes
it should be noted that although our own French playing cards are used,
the Tarot cards are also common in Spain. Cinema tickets as well as those
for the theatre are often bought in advance. There is a late cinema session
after dinner. Smoking in the auditorium is not usually allowed. Night
clubs are an exception to the generally moderate prices of refreshment in
Spain, although some good floor shows may be seen for the price of a
well-nursed long drink. If you are in Catalonia and feel like dancing you
may learn the *sardana* in the street of a fine evening.

VOCABULARY

Fishing, la pesca (páys-ka)
    bait, el cebo (tháy-bo)
    fish, el pez (peth)
    fisherman, el pescador (pays-ka-dhór)
    fly, la mosca (mós-ka)
    hook, el anzuelo (an-thoo-áy-lo)
    line, la línea (leé-nay-a)
    net, la red (red)
    permit, el permiso (per-mēē-so)
    river, el río (rēē-o)
    rod, la caña (kán-ya)
    salmon, el salmón (sal-món)
    stream, el arroyo (a-ró-yo)
    trout, la trucha (trōō-cha)
Golf, el golf
    ball, la pelota (pay-ló-ta)
    bunker, la hoya de arena (ó-ya day a-ráy-na)
    caddie, el caddie
    drive, el golpe de salida (gól-pay day sa-lēē-dha)
    fairway, el fairway
    flag, la bandera (ban-dáy-ra)
    golf bag, la bolsa (ból-sa)
    golf club, el palo (pá-lo)
    golf club (people), el club de golf
    golf course, el campo de golf (kám-po day golf)
    golfer, el jugador de golf (hoo-ga-dhór day golf)
    green, el green
    hole, el hoyo (ó-yo)
    iron, el acero (a-tháy-ro)
    putt, el tiro al hoyo (tēē-ro al ó-yo)
    putter, el putter
    swear word, el taco (tá-ko): a suitable one would be ¡Leche!
      (láy-chay)
    tee, la salida (sal-lēē-dha)
    wood, el madero (ma-dháy-ro)
Horse-racing, las carreras de caballos (ka-ráy-ras day ka-bál-yos)

Ski-ing, el esquí (es-kēē)
  chair-lift, la telesilla (tay-lay-sēēl-ya)
Tennis, el tenis (tén-ees)
  advantage: in, out, ventaja: dentro, fuera (ven-tá-ha: dén-tro, foo-áy-ra)
  backhand, la devolución de revés (day-vo-loo-thee-ón day ray-vés)
  ball, la pelota (pay-ló-ta)
  court, la pista de tenis (peés-ta day tén-ees)
  deuce, a dos (a dos)
  doubles, el doble (dó-blay)
  forehand, la devolución de derecho (day-vo-loo-thee-ón day day-ráy-cho)
  line, la línea (lēē-nay-a)
  lob, el lob
  love, cero (tháy-ro)
  match, el partido (par-tēē-dho)
  net, la red (red)
  racquet, la raqueta (ra-káy-ta)
  service, el saque (sá-kay)
  singles, el individual (een-dee-vee-dhoo-ál)
  thirty all, treinta tanto (tráy-een-ta tán-to)
  tournament, el torneo (tor-náy-o)
  volley, el golpe de voleo (gól-pay day vo-láy-o)

Can one go fishing here (there)? ¿Se puede pescar con caña aquí (allí)?
say poo-áy-dhay pays-kár kon kán-ya a-kēē (al-yēē)

What is the fishing like just now? ¿Cómo está la pesca en este momento?
kó-mo es-tá la páys-ka en és-tay mo-mén-to

Are there any big ones? ¿Los hay grandes?
los á-ee grán-days

Whose permission does one ask? ¿A quién se pide permiso?
a kee-én say pēē-dhay per-mēē-so

Is there a golf course? ¿Hay campo de golf?
á-ee kám-po day golf

How many holes has it? ¿Cuántos hoyos tiene?
kwán-tos ó-yos tee-áy-nay

Can strangers play? ¿Pueden jugar los forasteros?
poo-áy-dhen hoo-gár los fo-ras-táy-ros

I have brought my clubs.   He traído mis palos.
ay tra-ēē-dho mees pá-los

There are only nine holes.   No hay más que nueve hoyos.
no á-ee mas kay noo-áy-vay ó-yos

We are going to the races.   Vamos a las carreras.
vámos a las ka-ráy-ras

Is there a car park?   ¿Hay un estacionamiento para los coches?
á-ee ōōn es-ta-thee-o-na-mee-én-to pá-ra los kó-chays

We would like to play tennis.   Nos gustaría jugar al tenis.
nos goos-ta-rēē-a hoo-gár al ténis

I should like to play in the tournament.   Quisiera jugar en el torneo.
kee-see-áy-ra hoo-gár en el tor-náy-o

What is the score?   ¿Qué es el tanto?
kay es el tán-to

It is love-fifteen.   Estamos a cero a quince.
es-tá-mos a tháy-ro a kēēn-thay

That was a good one!   ¡Vale!
vá-lay

Whose service is it?   ¿A quién toca el saque?
a kee-én tó-ka el sá-kay

ENTERTAINMENT VOCABULARY

attendant, el(la) encargado(a) (en-kar-gá-dho/a)
ball, el baile de gala (bá-ee-lay day gá-la)
box (theatre), el palco (pál-ko)
box-office, la taquilla (ta-kēél-ya)
cinema, el cine (thēē-nay)
cloakroom, el guardarropa (gwar-da-ró-pa)
conductor, el director (dee-rek-tór)
dance, el baile (bá-ee-lay)
dancer: male, el bailarín (ba-ee-la-rēēn)
dancer: female, la bailarina (ba-ee-la-rēē-na)
dress circle, el principal (preen-thee-pál)
dubbed version, el doblaje (do-blá-hay)
evening dress, el traje de etiqueta (trá-hay day ay-tee-káy-ta)

exit (emergency), la salida (de urgencia) (sa-leé-dha day oor-hén-thee-a)
film, la película (pay-lēē-koo-la), el film (feelm)
foyer, la sala de descanso (sá-la day des-kán-so)
gallery, el paraíso (pa-ra-ēē-so)
interval, el descanso (des-kán-so)
light opera, la zarzuela (thar-thoo-áy-la)
music, la música (mōō-see-ka)
newsreel, el film de actualidades (ak-too-a-lee-dá-dhays), el "nodo" (nó-dho)
opera, la ópera (ó-pay-ra)
orchestra, la orquesta (or-káys-ta)
orchestra stalls, las butacas de patio (boo-tá-kas day pá-tee-o)
patrons, los concurrentes (kon-koo-rén-tays)
performance, la función (foon-thee-ón)
pit, el patio (pá-tee-o)
play, la pieza (pee-áy-tha), la comedia (ko-máy-dhee-a)
row, la fila (fēē-la)
screen, la pantalla (pan-tál-ya)
seat, la plaza (plá-tha), el sitio (sēē-tee-o)
show, el espectáculo (es-pek-tá-koo-lo)
stage, la escena (es-tháy-na)
stalls, el patio (pá-tee-o)
star, la estrella (es-trél-ya)
theatre, el teatro (tay-á-tro)
ticket, la entrada (en-trá-dha)
upper circle, el anfiteatro (an-fee-tay-á-tro)
usher, el acomodador (a-ko-mo-da-dhór)
waltz, el vals (vals)

Advance bookings.   Venta anticipada.
                               vén-ta an-tee-thee-pá-dha

Continuous performance.   Sesión continua.
                               say-see-ón kon-teé-noo-a

Air-conditioned.   Sala refrigerada.
                               sá-la ray-free-hay-rá-dha

Adults only.   Mayores.
                               ma-yó-rays

Suitable for all (for children).   Apto todos públicos (menores).
                               áp-to tó-dhos pōō-blee-kos (may-nó-rays)

Is it a good film?   ¿Es un buen film?
                               es oon boo-én feelm

I like that actor (actress).	Me gusta aquel actor (aquella actriz).

may gōōs-ta a-kél ak-tór (a-kél-ya ak-trēēth)

When does the next performance start?	¿Cuándo empieza la próxima función?

kwán-do em-pee-áy-tha la próx-ce-ma foon-thee-ón

Enjoy yourselves!	¡Que se diviertan!

kay say dee-vee-áyr-tan

Would you like to dance?	¿Quisiera usted bailar?

kee-see-áy-ra oos-táydh ba-ee-lár

I cannot dance this.	No sé bailar esto.

no say ba-ee-lár és-to

I'll teach you.	Se lo enseñaré.

say lo en-sen-ya-ráy

Should one wear evening dress?	¿Hay que llevar traje de etiqueta?

á-ee kay lyay-vár trá-hay day ay-tee-káy-ta

It is not necessary.	No hace falta.

no á-thay fál-ta

CAMPING AND WEATHER

Camping facilities are not so common in Spain as in France since hotel prices are more competitive and water is not so readily available. There are not as yet reciprocal arrangements for youth hostellers. Hiking and hitch-hiking are not entirely approved of by the police in sparsely patrolled areas.

VOCABULARY

air mattress, el colchón de aire (kol-chón day á-ee-ray)
blanket, la manta (mán-ta)
bucket, el cubo (kōō-bo)
camp, to, acampar (a-kam-pár)
camp bed, la cama tijera (ká-ma tee-háy-ra)
camping site, el terreno de camping (tay-ráy-no day kám-ping)
candle, la bujía (boo-hēē-a)
cloud, la nube (nōō-bay)
cold, el frío (frēē-o)
compass, la brújula (brōō-hoo-la)

cork-screw, el sacacorchos (sa-ka-kór-chos)
cup, la taza (tá-tha)
dawn, el amanecer (a-ma-nay-thér), el alba (ál-ba)
drinking water, el agua potable (á-gwa po-tá-blay)
dusk, el anochecer (a-no-chay-thér)
fire, el fuego (foo-áy-go), la lumbre (lōōm-bray)
firewood, la leña (láyn-ya)
first aid kit, el botiquín (bo-tee-kēēn)
fog, la niebla
frying pan. la sartén (sar-tén)
groundsheet, la alfombra (al-fóm-bra)
hail, el granizo (gra-nēē-tho)
heat, el calor (ka-lór)
hike, to, viajar a pie (vee-a-hár a pee-áy)
hitch-hike, to, viajar pidiendo ser llevado (vee-a-hár pee-dhee-én-do ser lyay-vá-dho)
ice, el hielo (ee-áy-lo)
lamp, la lámpara (lám-pa-ra)
latrine, la letrina (lay-trēē-na)
lightning, el relámpago (re-lám-pa-go)
matches, las cerillas (thay-rēēl-yas)
meadow, el prado (prá-dho)
methylated spirit, el alcohol para quemar (al-ko-ól pá-ra kay-már)
mist, la neblina (nay-blēē-na)
mud, el barro (bá-ro), el lodo (ló-dho)
paraffin, el petróleo (pay-tró-lay-o)
path, la senda (sáyn-da)
picnic, la comida campestre (ko-mēē-dha kam-páys-tray)
pillow, la almohada (al-mo-á-dha)
plate, el plato (plá-to)
pocket knife, la navaja de bolsillo (na-vá-ha day bol-sēēl-yo)
rain, la lluvia (lyōō-vee-a)
rubbish, la basura (ba-sōō-ra)
rucksack, la mochila (mo-chēē-la)
saucepan, la cacerola (ka-thay-ró-la)
shorts, el pantalón corto (pan-ta-lón kór-to)
shower, el chubasco (choo-bás-ko), el aguacero (a-gwa-tháy-ro)
sleeping bag, el saco de dormir (sá-ko day dor-mēēr)
snow, la nieve (nee-áy-vay)
storm, la tormenta (tor-mén-ta), la tempestad (tem-ρes-tádh)
stove, el anafe (a-náf-ay)
sun (shine), el sol (sol)
tent, la tienda (tee-áyn-da)
tent peg, el piquete (pee-káy-tay)
tent pole, el mastil (mas-tēēl)
tent rope, el cordón (kor-dón)
thunder, el trueno (troo-áy-no)
tin-opener, el abrelatas (a-bray-lá-tas)
toilet bag, el neceser (nay-thay-sér)
torch, la lámpara de bolsillo (lám-pa-ra day bol-sēēl-yo)

transistor radio, la radio portátil (rá-dhee-o por-tá-teel)
vacuum flask, la botella de vacío (bo-táyl-ya day va-thée-o)
water bottle, la cantimplora (kam-teem-pló-ra)
waterproof, impermeable (eem-per-may-á-blay)
weather, el tiempo (tee-ém-po)
wind, el viento (vee-én-to)

What is the weather like?   ¿Qué tiempo hace?
                                        kay tee-áym-po á-thay

The weather is good (bad).   Hace buen (mal) tiempo.
                                        á-thay boo-én (mal) tee-áym-po

It is clear (cloudy).   Está claro (nublado).
                                        es-tá klá-ro (noo-blá-dho)

The sun is shining.   Hace sol.
                                        á-thay sol

It is warm (cold, windy).   Hace calor (frío, viento).
                                        á-thay ka-lór (frée-o, vee-áyn-to)

**It is raining (drizzling, freezing, Llueve (llovizna, hiela, nieva).
snowing).**
                                        lyoo-áy-vay (lyo-véeth-na, ee-áy-la, nee-áy-va)

It is pouring with rain.   Llueve a cántaros.
                                        lyoo-áy-vay a kán-ta-ros

The sun is getting hot.   El sol empieza a picar.
                                        el sol em-pee-áy-tha a pee-kár

I can't stand the heat.   No aguanto el calor.
                                        no a-gwán-to el ka-lór

There is thunder (lightning).   Truena (relampaguea).
                                        troo-áy-na (ray-lam-pa-gáy-a)

It is getting light (dark).   Amanece (oscurece).
                                        a-ma-náy-thay (os-koo-ráy-thay)

Let's take shelter.   Si nos ponemos al abrigo.
                                        see nos po-náy-mos al a-brée-go

Let's go into the shade.   Vamos a la sombra.
                                        vá-mos a la sóm-bra

I'm soaked.   Estoy mojado hasta los huesos.
                                        es-tóy mo-há-dho á-sta los wáy-sos

I'm sweating.   Estoy sudando.
                                       es-tóy soo-dán-do

The temperature is . . . degrees   La temperatura es de . . . grados
above (below) zero.   sobre (bajo) cero.
  la tem-pay-ra-tōō-ra es day . . . grá-dhos só-bray (bá-ho) tháy-ro

What is the weather forecast?   ¿Qúe es el pronóstico mete-
                                         orológico?
  kay es el pro-nós-tee-ko may-tay-o-ro-ló-hee-ko

It is going to rain.   Va a llover.
                                       va a lyo-vér

It will be a fine day.   El día se promete bien.
  el dēē-a say pro-máy-tay bee-én

It will be a wet (dull) day.   Será un día lluvioso (cubierto).
  say-rá oon dēē-a lyoo-vee-ó-so (koo-bee-áyr-to)

Is there drinking water?   ¿Hay agua potable?
  á-ee á-gwa po-tá-blay

We are looking for a camping   Buscamos un terreno de
site.   camping.
  boos-ká-mos oon tay-ráy-no day kám-ping

Is camping allowed?   ¿Está autorizado el camping?
  es-tá ow-to-ree-thá-dho el kám-ping

Can we camp here?   ¿Se permite acampar aquí?
  say per-mēē-tay a-kam-pár a-kēē

Who is in charge of the site?   ¿Quién es el encargado del
                                         terreno?
  kee-én es el en-kar-gá-dho del tay-ráy-no

Whose permission must we ask?   ¿A quién debemos pedir
                                         permiso?
  a kee-én day-báy-mos pay-dhēēr per-mēē-so

May we light a fire?   ¿Se puede hacer un fuego?
  say poo-áy-dhay a-thér oon foo-áy-go

How much do you charge a day?   ¿Cuánto cobra usted al día?
  kwán-to kó-bra oos-táydh al dēē-a

Where can I buy . . . ?   ¿Dónde puedo comprar . . . ?
  dón-day poo-áy-dho kom-prár . . .

| **Where can I put this rubbish?** | ¿Dónde puedo echar esta basura? |

dón-day poo-áy-dho ay-chár és-ta ba-sōō-ra

| **We shall be leaving early.** | Nos marcharemos temprano. |

nos mar-char-áy-mos tem-prá-no

| **Can we pay now?** | ¿Cobrará usted ahora? |

ko-bra-rá oos-táydh a-ó-ra

SHOPPING

Shops are open from about 9 a.m. to 1 p.m. and from about 3.30 p.m. to about 8 p.m. Opening hours generally depend on the time of year, so that from May to October; when the *horario de verano* (o-rá-ree-o day vay-rá-no) or summer time-table is in operation, the afternoon break is longer and the evening closing hour correspondingly later. As a rule only food shops are open on Sundays. Sizes and measurements differ from those in use in Britain and the U.S.A. Tables of these continental sizes will be found in the appendix. Fruit and vegetables are sold by the *kilo* (kēē-lo), or *kilogramo*, which is about 2 lb. weight. Prices are normally given in pesetas but the following terms are also used; *un duro* (oon dōō-ro) = 5 *pesetas*; *un real* (oon ray-ál) = ¼ peseta or 25 *céntimos* (thén-tee-mos). Good value will be found among the following types of goods: leather-work, basket work, wrought iron work, lace, filigree work, sherries and liqueurs.

Shops: *Las tiendas* (tee-én-das)

baker, la panadería (pa-na-dhay-rēē-a)
    la pastelería (pas-tel-ay-rēē-a)
barber, la barbería (bar-bay-rēē-a)
bookshop, la librería (lee-bray-rēē-a)
chemist, la farmacia (far-má-thee-a)
cleaner, dyer, la tintorería (teen-to-ray-rēē-a)
confectioner, la confitería (kon-fee-tay-rēē-a)
dairy, la lechería (lay-chay-rēē-a)
department store, el almacén (al-ma-thén)
draper, tejidos y confecciones (tay-hēē-dos ee kon-fek-thee-ó-nays)
dressmaker, la modista (mo-dhēēs-ta)
fancy leather goods, artículos de cuero (ar-tēē-koo-los day kwáy-ro)
fishmonger, la pescadería (pes-ca-dhay-rēē-a)
fruiterer, la frutería (froo-tay-rēē-a)

grocer, alimentación (a-lee-men-ta-thee-ón)
      comestibles (ko-mes-tēē-blays)
      ultramarinos (ool-tra-ma-rēē-nos)
hairdresser, la peluquería (pay-loo-kay-rēē-a)
ironmonger, la ferretería (fay-ray-tay-rēē-a)
jeweller, la joyería (ho-yay-rēē-a)
laundry, el lavado de ropa (la-vá-dho day ró-pa)
newsagent, el estanco (es-tán-ko), el puesto de periódicos (poo-áys-to day pay-ree-ó-dhee-kos)
optician, el óptico (óp-tee-ko)
perfumery, la perfumería (per-foo-may-rēē-a)
photographic dealer, la fotografía (fo-to-gra-fēē-a)
pork-butcher, la salchichería (sal-chee-chay-rēē-a)
shirtmaker, la camisería (ka-mee-say-rēē-a)
shoemaker (repairs), salón de limpiabotas (sa-lón day lēēm-pee-a-bó-tas) zapatero remendón (tha-pa-táy-ro ray-men-dón)
shoe-shop, calzado (kal-thá-dho), la zapatería (tha-pa-tay-rēē-a)
stationer, la papelería (pa-pay-lay-rēē-a)
tailor, la sastrería (sas-tray-rēē-a)
tobacconist, el estanco (es-tán-ko)

VOCABULARY

battery, la batería (ba-tay-rēē-a)
book, el libro (lēē-bro)
cheap, barato (ba-rá-to)
cigarette, el cigarillo (thee-ga-rēēl-yo), el pitillo (pee-tēēl-yo)
counter, el mostrador (mos-tra-dhór)
dear, caro (ká-ro)
dictionary, el diccionario (deek-thee-on-á-ree-o)
discount, la rebaja (ray-bá-ha)
doll, el muñeco (la muñeca) (moon-yáy-ko/ka)
elastic, elástico (ay-lás-tee-ko)
envelope, el sobre (só-bray)
gramophone record, el disco (dēēs-ko)
guide book, la guía (gēē-a)
handbag, el bolso (ból-so)
ink, la tinta (tēēn-ta)
label, la etiqueta (ay-tee-káy-ta)
magazine, la revista (ray-vēēs-ta)
map, el mapa (má-pa)
market, el mercado (mayr-ká-dho)
matches, las cerillas (thay-rēēl-yas)
nail-file, la lima de uñas (lēē-ma day ōōn-yas)
needle, la aguja (a-gōō-ha)
newspaper, el periódico (pay-ree-ó-dhee-ko), el diario (dee-á-ree-o)

pen, ball-point, el bolígrafo (bo-lēē-gra-fo)
pencil, el lápiz (lá-peeth)
pin, el alfiler (al-fee-lér)
pin, safety, el imperdible (eem-per-dēē-blay)
purse, el portamonedas (por-ta-mo-náy-dhas)
ring, la sortija (sor-tēē-ha)
sale, la venta (váyn-ta)
scissors, las tijeras (tee-háy-ras)
shoe-laces, los cordones para zapatos (kor-dó-nays pá-ra
      tha-pá-tos)
shopkeeper, el tendero (tayn-dáy-ro)
string, el bramante (bra-mán-tay)
sweets, los caramelos (ka-ra-máy-los)
thread, el hilo (ēē-lo)
toy, el juguete (hoo-gáy-tay)
umbrella, el paraguas (pa-rá-gwas)
wallet, la cartera (car-táy-ra)
watch, el reloj (ray-lóh)
writing-paper, el papel de escribir (pa-pél day es-kree-bēēr)

Where can I buy . . . ?	¿Dónde puedo comprar . . . ? dón-day poo-áy-dho kom-prár . . .
Have you any . . . ?	¿Tiene usted . . . ? tee-áy-nay oos-táydh
Have you any British (American) cigarettes?	¿Tiene usted cigarillos ingleses (americanos)? tee-áy-nay oos-táydh thee-ga-rēēl-yos een-gláy-says (a-may-ree-ká-nos)
At what time do the shops open?	¿A qué hora se abren las tiendas? a kay ó-ra say á-bren las tee-én-das
Where are the best shops?	¿Dónde están las mejores tiendas? dón-day es-tán las may-hó-rays tee-én-das
How much is it?	¿Cuánto es? kwán-to es
Would you write down the price?	¿Sírvase escribir el precio? sēēr-va-say es-kree-bēēr el práy-thee-o
How much (how many) do you want?	¿Cuánto (cuántos) quiere usted? kwán-to(s) kee-áy-ray oos-táydh

A pound of grapes please.	Medio kilo de uvas, por favor. máy-dhee-o kēē-lo day ōō-vas por fa-vór
Do you have change?	¿ Tiene usted el cambio? tee-áy-nay oos-táydh el kám-bee-o
Have you anything cheaper?	¿ Tiene usted algo más barato? tee-áy-nay oos-táydh ál-go mas ba-rá-to
It is too expensive.	Es demasiado caro. es day-ma-see-á-dho ká-ro
Have you something of better quality?	¿ Tiene usted algo de mejor calidad? tee-áy-nay oos-táydh ál-go day may-hór ka-lee-dhádh
Pay at the cash-desk, please.	Sírvase pagar a la caja. sēēr-va-say pa-gár a la ká-ha
You have given me the wrong change.	Se ha equivocado con el cambio. say a ay-kee-vo-ká-dho kon el kám-bee-o
I bought this yesterday.	Compré esto ayer. kom-práy és-to a-yér
It doesn't work.	No funciona. no foon-thee-ó-na
Can you change it?	¿ Puede usted darme otro? poo-áy-dhay oos-táydh dár-may ó-tro
Can you refund my money?	¿ Puede usted reintegrármelo? poo-áy-dhay oos-táydh ray-een-tay-grár-may-lo
Can you send it?	¿ Puede usted mandarlo? poo-áy-dhay oos-táydh man-dár-lo
Will you accept a traveller's cheque?	¿ Aceptará usted un cheque de viajero? a-thayp-ta-rá oos-táydh oon cháy-kay day vee-a-háy-ro
Do you sell . . . ?	¿ Vende usted . . . ? váyn-day oos-táydh . . .
May I come back and collect it?	¿ Puedo volver a recogerlo? poo-áy-dho vol-vér a ray-ko-hér-lo
I want something similar to this.	Deseo algo parecido a esto. day-sáy-o ál-go pa-ráy-thēē-dho a és-to

Have you anything bigger   ¿ Tiene usted algo más grande
(smaller, thicker, thinner)?   (pequeño, grueso, delgado)?
tee-áy-nay oos-táydh ál-go mas grán-day (pay-káyn-yo, groo-áy-so, del-gá-dho)

Can you wrap it up?   ¿ Puede usted envolverlo?
poo-áy-dhay oos-táydh en-vol-vér-lo

Have you a paper bag?   ¿ Tiene usted un saco de papel?
tee-áy-nay oos-táydh oon sá-ko day pa-pél

I need ...   Necesito ...
nay-thay-sée-to ...

I (do not) like it.   (No) me gusta.
(no) may gōōs-ta

You have not sent ...   No ha mandado ...
no a man-dá-dho ...

Here is my address.   He aquí mis señas.
ay a-kée mees sáyn-yas

Do you sell long-playing   ¿ Vende usted discos de larga
records?   duración?
vén-day oos-táydh dēēs-kos day lár-ga doo-ra-thee-ón

POST OFFICE

Tobacconists' kiosks which sell postage stamps and receive mail for
posting are painted red and yellow, as are pillar and post boxes. Other
business has to be transacted at a main post office. When posting mail
abroad use the box marked *extranjero* (ex-tran-háy-ro), foreign mail.

VOCABULARY

address, la dirección (dee-rek-thee-ón), las señas (sáyn-yas)
airmail, el correo aéreo (ko-ráy-o a-áy-ray-o)
cablegram, el cablegrama (ka-blay-grá-ma)
collection, la recogida (ray-ko-hēē-dha)
delivery, la distribución (dees-tree-boo-thee-ón)
express, urgente (oor-hén-tay)
letter, la carta (kár-ta)
mail, el correo (ko-ráy-o)
parcel, el paquete (pa-káy-tay)
post box, el buzón (boo-thón)
post office, la casa de correos (ká-sa day ko-ráy-os)

postal order, el giro postal (hēē-ro pos-tál)
postcard, la tarjeta postal (tar-háy-ta pos-tál)
postman, el cartero (kar-táy-ro)
reply coupon, el cupón de respuesta (koo-pón day res-poo-áys-ta)
sign, to, firmar (feer-már)
telegram, el telegrama (tay-la-grá-ma)

Where is the Post Office?	¿Dónde está la Casa de Correos?
	dón-day es-tá la ká-sa day ko-ráy-os
I want some stamps.	Quiero sellos.
	kee-áy-ro sáyl-yos
How much is it to send a letter (postcard) abroad?	¿Cuánto es una carta (una postal) al extranjero?
	kwán-to es ōō-na kár-ta (ōō-na pos-tál) al ex-tran-háy-ro
Will this go tonight?	¿Saldrá esta noche?
	sal-drá és-ta nó-chay
I want to send this parcel.	Quiero mandar este paquete.
	kee-áy-ro man-dár és-tay pa-káy-tay
I want to register it.	Quiero certificarlo.
	kee-áy-ro ther-tee-fee-kár-lo
Where are there telegraph forms?	¿Dónde hay impresos de telegrama?
	dón-day á-ee eem-práy-sos day tay-lay-grá-ma
Where can I cash a postal order?	¿Dónde se cobran los giros?
	dón-day say kó-bran los hēē-ros
Where is the Poste Restante?	¿Dónde está la Lista de Correos?
	dón-day es-tá la lēēs-ta day ko-ráy-os
Is there a letter for me?	¿Hay una carta para mi?
	á-ee ōō-na kár-ta pá-ra mēē
Have you any identification papers?	¿Tiene usted alguna pieza de identificación?
	tee-áy-nay oos-táydh al-gōō-na pee-áy-tha day ee-dhen-tee-fee-ka-thee-ón

I want to send a telegram.　　　　Quiero poner un telegrama.
kee-áy-ro po-nér oon tay-lay-grá-ma

How much is it per word?　　　　¿Cuánto es por palabra?
kwán-to es por pa-lá-bra

THE TELEPHONE

Numbers should be stated individually, e.g. 707 = *siete, cero, siete*. The telephone and postal buildings are often separate. One may telephone from a bar on buying a jeton, *ficha* (fee-cha), which is put in the slot to pay for a call. Some delay may be experienced in having a trunk call put through.

VOCABULARY

call, la comunicación (ko-moo-nee-ka-thee-ón), la llamada (lya-má-dha)
dial, to, marcar (mar-kár)
directory, la guía de teléfonos (gēē-a day tay-láy-fo-nos)
exchange, la central (then-trál)
number, el número (nōō-may-ro)
operator, la señorita (sayn-yo-rēē-ta)
receiver, el auricular (ow-ree-koo-lár)
telephone, el teléfono (tay-láy-fo-no)
trunk call, la conferencia (kon-fay-rén-thee-a)

Where may I telephone?　　　　¿Dónde puedo telefonear?
dón-day poo-áy-dho tay-lay-fo-nay-ár

Is there a telephone?　　　　¿Hay el teléfono?
á-ee el tay-láy-fo-no

Operator, get me ...　　　　Señorita, por favor póngame...
sayn-yo-rēē-ta, por fav-ór pón-ga-may ...

I should like to make a trunk call to ...　　　　Quisiera una conferencia con ...
kee-see-áy-ra ōō-na kon-fay-rén-thee-a kon ...

Hullo! (making the call) (taking the call).　　　　¡Oiga! ¡Dígame!
óy-ga, dēē-ga-may

There is no answer.　　　　No contestan.
no kon-táys-tan

The line is engaged.   Está comunicando.
                                es-tá ko-moo-nee-kán-do

This is Mr. Smith.   Es el Señor Smith.
                            el el sayn-yór Smith

Is Mr. Quevedo at home?   ¿Está el Señor Quevedo?
                            es-tá el sayn-yór Quevedo

He is not at home.   No está.
                                no es-tá

Will you take a message?   ¿Quiere usted tomar un
                                    mensaje?
                      kee-áy-ray oos-táydh to-már oon men-sá-hay

Ask him to ring me.   Dígale que me llame.
                            dēē-ga-lay kay may lyá-may

CHEMIST

Chemists do not sell such a wide range of articles as in Britain and for
perfumes and soap, for instance, one would go to a *perfumería*.   The
newspapers indicate which chemists' shops are open all night on a particular
date;   these are called the *farmacias de guardia* (day gwár-dee-a).

VOCABULARY

adhesive dressing, las tiritas (tee-rēē-tas)
aspirin, la aspirina (as-pee-rēē-na)
bandage, la venda (váyn-da)
chemist, la farmacia (far-má-thee-a)
cosmetics, los artículos de tocada (ar-tēē-koo-los day to-ká-dha)
cough sweets, las pastillas para la tos (pas-tēēl-yas pá-ra la tos)
disinfectant, el desinfectante (days-een-fek-tán-tay)
gargle, las gárgaras (gár-gar-as)
laxative, el laxante (lax-án-tay)
lint, las hilas (ēē-las)
lipstick, el lápiz de labios (lá-peeth day lá-bee-os)
medicine, el remedio (ray-máy-dhee-o), el medicamento (may-dhee-
    ka-mén-to)
nail brush, el cepillo de uñas (thay-pēēl-yo day ōōn-yas)
ointment, el ungüento (oon-gwén-to)
perfume, el perfume (per-fōō-may)
pill, la píldora (pēēl-do-ra)
powder, los polvos (pól-vos)
prescription, la receta (ray-tháy-ta)

quinine, la quinina (kee-nēē-na)
sanitary towels, las compresas higiénicas (kom-práy-sas ee-hee-áy-nee-kas)
sleeping pill, un somnífero (som-nēē-fay-ro)
soap, el jabón (ha-bón)
sponge, la esponja (es-pón-ha)
sunburn cream, la crema contra el sol (kráy-ma kón-tra el sol)
suntan lotion, el aceite para broncear (a-tháy-ee-tay pá-ra bron-thay-ár)
tablet, el comprimido (kom-pree-mēē-dho)
toilet paper, el papel higiénico (pa-pél ee-hee-áy-nee-ko)
tooth brush, el cepillo de dientes (thay-pēēl-yo day dee-én-tays)
toothpaste, el dentífrico (den-tēē-free-ko)

Can you make up this prescription?	¿Puede usted hacer esta receta?
	poo-áy-dhay oos-táydh a-thér és-ta ray-tháy-ta
I shall call for it later.	Volveré a recogerla.
	vol-vay-ráy a ray-ko-háyr-la
Can you read an English prescription?	¿Sabe usted leer una receta inglesa?
	sá-bay oos-táydh lay-ér ōō-na ray-tháy-ta een-gláy-sa
My back is badly sunburnt.	Tengo la espalda muy quemada del sol.
	tén-go la es-pál-da mwee kay-má-dha del sol
Give me something for mosquito bites.	Déme algo contra las picaduras de mosquito.
	dáy-may ál-go kón-tra las pee-ka-dhōō-ras day mos-kēē-to
Can you give me something for constipation (diarrhoea, hay fever)?	¿Puede usted darme algo contra el estreñimiento (la diarrea, la fiebre del heno)?
	poo-áy-dhay oos-táydh dár-may ál-go kón-tra el es-tren-yee-mee-én-to (la dee-a-ráy-a, la fee-áy-bray del áy-no)
Three times a day. In a glass of water.	Tres veces al día. En un vaso de agua.
	trays váy-thays al dēē-a. en oon vá-so day á-gwa
After meals.	Después de comer.
	days-poo-áys day ko-mér

Directions for use.   Modo de usar.
                                    mó-dho day oo-sár

For external use.   Para el uso externo.
                                   pá-ra el ōō-so ex-tér-no

HAIRDRESSER

VOCABULARY

MEN

after shave lotion, la loción de después del afeitado (lo-thee-ón
  day des-poo-áys del a-fay-ee-tá-dho)
barber's shop, la barbería (bar-bay-rēē-a)
beard, la barba (bár-ba)
comb, el peine (páy-ee-nay)
eau de Cologne, la colonia (ko-ló-nee-a)
hair, el pelo (páy-lo), los cabellos (ka-bél-yos)
hair cream, la crema para el pelo (kráy-ma pá-ra el páy-lo)
hair oil, la brillantina (breel-yan-tēē-na)
haircut, el corte de pelo (kór-tay day páy-lo)
hairdresser (men's), la barbería (bar-bay-rēē-a)
parting, la raya (rá-ya)
razor (safety), la máquina de afeitar (má-kee-na day a-fay-ee-tár)
razor blade, la hoja de afeitar (ó-ha day a-fay-ee-tár)
shampoo, el lavado de la cabeza (la-vá-dho day la ka-báy-tha)
shaver, electric, la máquina eléctrica de afeitarse (má-kee-na ay-lék-
  tree-ka day a-fay-ee-tár-say)
shaving brush, la brocha de afeitar (bró-cha day a-fay-ee-tár)
shaving cream, la crema de afeitar (kráy-ma day a-fay-ee-tár)
shaving stick, el jabón de afeitar (ha-bón day a-fay-ee-tár)

Shave please.   Sírvase afeitarme.
                                  sēēr-va-say a-fay-ee-tár-may

Haircut please.   Sírvase cortarme el pelo.
                                  sēēr-va-say kor-tár-may el páy-lo

Short back and sides.   Corto por detrás y al lado.
                                  kór-to por day-trás ee al lá-dho

A trim please.   Recórtelo por favor.
                                  ray-kór-tay-lo por fa-vór

A shampoo please.   Sírvase lavarme la cabeza.
                                  sēēr-va-say la-vár-may la ka-báy-tha

Shall I put anything on it?   ¿Le pongo algo?
lay pón-go ál-go

A little cologne.   Un poco de colonia.
oon pó-ko day ko-ló-nee-a

That's you then, sir.   ¡Servido, caballero!
ser-vēē-dho, ka-bal-yáy-ro

Something else? Nothing else.   ¿Algo más? Nada más.
ál-go mas. ná-dha mas

WOMEN

appointment, la cita (thēē-ta)
comb, el peine (páy-ee-nay)
curl, el rizo (rēē-tho)
curler, el rizador (ree-tha-dhór)
dryer, el secador (say-ka-dhór)
dye, el tinte para el pelo (tēēn-tay pá-ra el páy-lo)
hair, el pelo (páy-lo), los cabellos (ka-bél-yos)
hairdresser, el(la) peluquero(a) (pay-loo-káy-ro/ra)
hairnet, la redecilla (ray-dhay-thēēl-ya)
hairpin, la horquilla (or-kēēl-ya)
lacquer, la laca (lá-ka)
permanent wave, la permanente (per-ma-nén-tay)
wave, la onda (ón-da)
wig, la peluca (pay-lōō-ka)

May I make an appointment?   ¿Puede usted darme cita?
poo-áy-dhay oos-táydh dár-may thēē-ta

I want my hair trimmed.   Córteme un poco el pelo.
cór-tay-may oon pó-ko el páy-lo

Not too short.   No demasiado corto.
no day-ma-see-á-dho kór-to

Quite short.   Bastante corto.
bas-tán-tay kór-to

Don't take any off the top.   No corte nada de arriba.
no kór-tay ná-dha day a-rēē-ba

I want a manicure.   Deseo una manicura.
day-sáy-o ōō-na ma-nee-kōō-ra

I want my hair tinted.   Deseo teñirme el pelo.
day-sáy-o ten-yēēr-may el páy-lo

The same colour (darker, El mismo color (más oscuro,
   lighter).   más claro).
     el mēēs-mo ko-lór (mas os-kōō-ro, mas klá-ro)

A shampoo and set, please. Lavar y marcar, por favor.
         la-vár ee mar-kár, por fa-vór

It is too hot. Está demasiado caliente.
       es-tá day-ma-see-á-dho ka-lee-én-tay

I have dry (greasy) hair. Tengo el pelo seco (grasiento).
       tén-go el páy-lo sáy-ko (gra-see-én-to)

I would like a cold (hot) perm. Quisiera una permanente en
                     frío (caliente).
     kee-see-áy-ra ōō-na per-ma-nén-tay en frēē-o (ka-lee-én-tay)

PHOTOGRAPHY

VOCABULARY

camera, el aparato fotográfico (a-pa-rá-to fo-to-grá-fee-ko)
enlargement, la ampliación (am-plee-a-thee-ón)
film (colour), la cinta de color (thēēn-ta day ko-lór)
film (miniature), la cinta en miniatura (thēēn-ta en mee-nee-a-tōō-ra)
filter, el filtro de luz (fēēl-tro day looth)
flash bulb, la bombilla relámpago (bom-bēēl-ya ray-lám-pa-go)
lens, el objetivo (ob-hay-tēē-vo)
lens hood, el capuchón (ka-poo-chón)
light meter, el exposímetro (ex-po-sēē-may-tro)
negative, la prueba negativa (proo-áy-ba nay-ga-tēē-va)
photograph, la fotografía (fo-to-gra-fēē-a)
print, la copia (kó-pee-a)
range finder, el telémetro (tay-láy-may-tro)
shutter, el obturador (ob-too-ra-dhór)
slide, la diapositiva (dee-a-po-see-tēē-va)
snapshot, la instantánea (een-stan-tá-nay-a)
stereoscope, el estereoscopio (es-tay-ray-o-skó-pee-o)
view finder, el visor (vee-sór)
winder, el enrollador (en-rol-ya-dhór)

Have you a fast (colour) film? ¿Tiene usted una película
                            rápida de color)?
     tee-áy-nay oos-taydh ōō-na pay-lēē-koo-la rá-pee-dha (day co-lór)

What size do you want?	¿Qué tamaño quiere?
	kay ta-mán-yo kee-áy-ray
Will you develop this film please.	Haga el favor de revelar esta película.
	á-ga el fa-vór day ray-vay-lár és-ta pay-lēē-koo-la
When will it be ready?	¿Cuándo estará?
	kwán-do es-ta-rá
I want two prints of each negative.	Deseo dos copias de cada prueba.
	day-sáy-o dos kó-pee-as day ká-dha proo-áy-ba
Please enlarge this.	Amplíe esto, por favor.
	am-plēē-ay és-to por fa-vór
They are under-exposed.	No las ha revelado bastante.
	no las a ray-vay-lá-dho bas-tán-tay
They are over-exposed.	Las ha revelado demasiado.
	las a ray-vay-lá-dho day-mas-ee-á-dho
The film is jammed.	La cinta está atascada.
	la thēēn-ta es-tá a-tas-ká-dha
The winder isn't working.	El enrollador no funciona.
	el en-rol-ya-dhór no foon-thee-ó-na

CLOTHING

VOCABULARY

MEN

belt, el cinturón (theen-too-rón)
bow-tie, la corbata de lazo (kor-bá-ta day lá-tho)
braces, los tirantes de pantalón (tee-rán-tays day pan-ta-lón)
button, el botón (bo-tón)
cap, la gorra (gó-ra)
collar, el cuello (koo-él-yo)
collar stud, el pasador (pa-sa-dhór)
cuff links, las gemelas (hay-máy-las)
dinner jacket, el smoking
dressing gown, la bata (bá-ta)
evening dress, el traje de etiqueta (trá-hay day ay-tee-káy-ta)
gloves, los guantes (goo-án-tays)
handkerchief, el pañuelo (pan-yoo-áy-lo)
hat, el sombrero (som-bráy-ro)
jacket, la chaqueta (cha-káy-ta)

jersey, el jersey (her-sáy)
overcoat, el abrigo (a-brēē-go)
pyjamas, el pijama (pee-há-ma)
raincoat, el impermeable (eem-per-may-á-blay), la gabardina (ga-bar-dēē-na)
sandals, las sandalias (san-dá-lee-as), las alpargatas (al-par-gá-tas)
shirt, la camisa (ka-mēē-sa)
shoes, los zapatos (tha-pá-tos), el calzado (kal-thá-dho)
slippers, las zapatillas (tha-pa-tēēl-yas)
socks, los calcetines (kal-thay-tēē-nays)
suit, el traje (trá-hay)
tie, la corbata (kor-bá-ta)
trousers, el pantalón (pan-ta-lón)
underpants, el calzoncillo (kal-thon-thēēl-yo)
vest, la camiseta (ka-mee-sáy-ta)
waistcoat, el chaleco (cha-láy-ko)

WOMEN

belt, el cinturón (theen-too-rón)
blouse, la blusa (blōō-sa)
bracelet, el brazalete (bra-tha-láy-tay)
brassiere, el sostén (sos-tén)
brooch, el broche (bró-chay)
button, el botón (bo-tón)
cloth, el paño (pán-yo)
coat, la chaqueta (cha-káy-ta)
corset, el corsé (kor-sáy)
cotton, el algodón (al-go-dhón)
dress, el vestido (ves-tēē-dho), el traje (trá-hay)
dressing-gown, la bata (bá-ta)
ear-rings, los pendientes (pen-dee-én-tays)
fine, fino (fēē-no)
frock, el vestido (ves-tēē-dho)
girdle, la faja (fá-ha)
gloves, las guantes (goo-án-tays)
gown, el traje de tarde (trá-hay day tár-day)
handkerchief, el pañuelo (pan-yoo-áy-lo)
hat, el sombrero (som-bráy-ro)
headscarf, el pañuelo de cabeza (pan-yoo-áy-lo day ka-báy-tha)
jacket, la chaqueta (cha-káy-ta)
jumper, el jersey (her-sáy)
lace, el encaje (en-ká-hay)
lingerie, la ropa interior (ró-pa een-tay-ree-ór)
loose, holgado (ol-gá-dho), flotante (flo-tán-tay)
low neck, el escote (es-kó-tay)
necklace, el collar (kol-yár)
nightdress, la camisa de dormir (ka-mēē-sa day dor-mēēr)
nylon, el nilón (nee-lón)

panties, las bragas (brá-gas)
petticoat, el enaguas (en-á-gwas)
pyjamas, el pijama (pee-há-ma)
rayon, el rayón (ray-ón)
scarf, la bufanda (boo-fán-da)
shawl, el mantón (man-tón)
shoes, los zapatos (tha-pá-tos)
skirt, la falda (fál-da)
silk, la seda (sáy-dha)
slip, la combinación (kom-bee-na-thee-ón)
stockings, las medias (máy-dhee-as)
suit, el traje (trá-hay)
suspender, el tirante de media (tee-rán-tay day máy-dhee-a)
suspender-belt, el porta-ligas (pór-ta-lēē-gas)
wool, la lana (lá-na)
zip, el cierre relámpago (thee-áy-ray ray-lám-pa-go)

What is your size?	¿Cuál es su tamaño?
	kwal es soo ta-mán-yo
The English size is . . .	La medida inglesa es de . . .
	la may-dhēē-dha een-gláy-sa es day
Can you match this colour?	¿Puede usted aparear este color?
	poo-áy-dhay oos-táydh a-pa-ray-ár és-tay ko-lór
May I see this by daylight?	¿Puedo verlo a la luz del día?
	poo-áy-dho vér-lo a la looth del dēē-a
I (do not) like this colour.	(No) me gusta este color.
	(no) may gŏŏs-ta és-tay ko-lór
I prefer that one.	Me gusta más ése.
	may gŏŏs-ta mas áy-say
I prefer a lighter (darker) colour.	Prefiero un color más claro (más oscuro).
	pray-fee-áy-ro oon ko-lór mas klá-ro (mas os-kŏŏ-ro)
Will it fade?	¿Se perderá el color?
	say per-day-rá el ko-lór
Will it shrink?	¿Se encogerá?
	say en-ko-hay-rá
May I try it on?	¿Puedo probármelo?
	poo-áy-dho pro-bár-may-lo

It is too big (small, loose, tight, long, short).
Es demasiado grande (pequeño, holgado, justo, largo, corto).
es day-ma-see-á-dho grán-day (pay-káyn-yo, ol-gá-dho, hōōs-to, lár-go, kór-to)

How long would you take to make me a suit?
¿Cuánto tardaría en hacerme un traje?
kwán-to tar-da-rēē-a en a-thér-may oon trá-hay

It does not fit me.
No me sienta bien.
no may see-áyn-ta bee-én

Can you alter it?
¿Puede usted modificarlo?
poo-áy-dhay oos-táydh mo-dhee-fee-kár-lo

REPAIRS

VOCABULARY

heel, el tacón (ta-kón)
key, la llave (lyá-vay)
lock, la cerradura (thay-ra-dhōō-ra)
sole, la suela (soo-áy-la)
spring, la cuerda (kwér-da)
strap, la correa (ko-ráy-a)
watch, el reloj (ray-ló)

I have broken, torn . . .
He roto . . .
ay ró-to . . .

I dropped it.
Se me cayó.
say may ka-yó

Can you repair . . . ?
¿Puede usted arreglar . . . ?
poo-áy-dhay oos-táydh a-ray-glár . . .

How long will it take?
¿Cuánto tardará?
kwán-to tar-da-rá

Will it be expensive?
¿Costará mucho?
kos-ta-rá mōō-cho

I need new lenses (frame)
Necesito nuevos cristales (una nueva montura).
nay-thay-sēē-to noo-áy-vos krees-tá-lays (noo-áy-va mon-tōō-ra)

My watch won't go.
Mi reloj no anda.
mee ray-ló no án-da

It gains (loses).	Adelanta (retrasa).

a-dhay-lán-ta (ray-trá-sa)

Can you let me have it back by . . . ?	¿ Puede usted devolvérmelo para . . . ?

poo-áy-dhay oos-táydh de-vol-vér-may-lo pá-ra . . .

I need new soles (heels)	Necisito suelas nuevas (tacones nuevos).

nay-thay-sēē-to soo-áy-las noo-áy-vas (ta-kó-nays noo-áy-vos)

Can you patch it?	¿ Puede ponerlo un remiendo?

poo-áy-dhay po-nér-lo oon ray-mee-én-do

Can you sew it?	¿ Puede coserlo?

poo-áy-dhay ko-sér-lo

ACCIDENTS AND ILLNESS

Most drugs except morphia, etc., can be obtained from chemists without a prescription It is useful to take with one a bottle of Mist. kaolin et Morph. (no prescription needed in Great Britain) as it is the best first aid for summer diarrhoea. Chemists often give good advice as well as first aid if needed. The fees of G.P.'s and specialists are reasonable but not many speak English. Dentists in Spain are also qualified doctors. Many small towns are served by non-resident dentists who visit the town two or three days a week. If you are not a regular patient the doctor or dentist will expect his fee on the spot.

VOCABULARY

PARTS OF THE BODY

ankle, el tobillo (to-bēēl-yo)
arm, el brazo (brá-tho)
back, la espalda (es-pál-da)
blood, la sangre (sán-gray)
bone, el hueso (wáy-so)
bowel, los intestinos (een-tes-tēē-nos)
cheek, la mejilla (may-hēēl-ya)
chest, el pecho (páy-cho)
chin, la barbilla (bar-bēēl-ya)
dentures, la dentadura (dayn-ta-dhōō-ra)
ear, la oreja (o-ráy-ha)
elbow, el codo (kó-dho)
eye, el ojo (ó-ho)
eyelid, el párpado (pár-pa-dho)
face, la cara (ká-ra)
finger, el dedo (dáy-dho)

S.P.B.---E

foot, el pie (pee-áy)
gum, la encía (en-thēē-a)
hand, la mano (má-no)
head, la cabeza (ka-báy-tha)
heart, el corazón (ko-ra-thón)
heel, el talón (ta-lón)
hip, la cadera (ka-dháy-ra)
joint, la articulación (ar-tee-koo-la-thee-ón)
kidney, el riñón (reen-yón)
knee, la rodilla (ro-dhēēl-ya)
knee-cap, la rodillera (ro-dheel-yáy-ra)
leg, la pierna (pee-áyr-na)
lip, el labio (lá-bee-o)
liver, el hígado (ēē-ga-dho)
lung, el pulmón (pool-món)
mouth, la boca (bó-ka)
neck, el cuello (koo-áyl-yo)
nerve, el nervio (náyr-vee-o)
nose, la nariz (na-rēēth)
shoulder, el hombro (óm-bro)
stomach, el estómago (es-tó-ma-go), el vientre (vee-áyn-tray)
throat, la garganta (gar-gán-ta)
toe, el dedo del pie (dáy-dho del pee-áy)
tongue, la lengua (lén-gwa)
tooth, el diente (dee-én-tay), la muela (moo-áy-la)
wrist, la muñeca (moon-yáy-ka)

GENERAL

abscess, el absceso (abs-tháy-so)
accident, el accidente (ak-thee-dháyn-tay)
ambulance, la ambulancia (am-boo-lán-thee-a)
appendicitis, la apendecitis (a-pen-day-thēē-tees)
bandage, la venda (váyn-da)
bite, el mordisco (mor-dēēs-ko)
blister, la ampolla (am-pól-ya)
boil, el furúnculo (foo-rōōn-koo-lo)
bruise, la contusión (kon-too-see-ón)
burn, la quemadura (kay-ma-dhōō-ra)
   heart-burn, la acedía (a-thay-dhēē-a)
   sun-burn, la quemadura del sol (kay-ma-dhōō-ra del sol)
chill, el resfriado (rays-free-á-dho)
chiropodist, el callista (kal-yēēs-ta)
cold, el constipado (kon-stee-pá-dho)
constipation, el estreñimiento (es-tren-yee-mee-én-to)
convalescence, la convalecencia (kon-va-lay-thén-thee-a)
cough, la tos (tos)
cramp, el entumecimiento (en-too-may-thee-mee-én-to)
cure, la cura (kōō-ra), el remedio (ray-máy-dhee-o)
cut, la cuchillada (koo-cheel-yá-dha)

dentist, el dentista (dayn-tēēs-ta)
diarrhoea, la diarrea (dee-a-ráy-a)
doctor, el médico (máy-dhee-ko)
emergency service, el servicio de urgencia (sayr-vēē-thee-o day oor-hén-thee-a)
epidemic, el epidémico (ay-pee-dháy-mee-ko)
faint, el desmayo (days-má-yo)
fever, la fiebre (fee-áy-bray)
filling, la orificación (o-ree-fee-ka-thee-ón)
    la empastadura (em-pas-ta-dhōō-ra)
fracture, la fractura (frak-tōō-ra)
hay-fever, el romadizo (ro-ma-dhēē-tho)
hospital, el hospital (os-pee-tál)
illness, la enfermedad (en-fer-may-dhádh)
indigestion, la indigestión (een-dee-hes-tee-ón)
influenza, la gripe (grēē-pay)
injection, la inyección (een-yek-thee-ón)
insomnia, el insomnio (een-sóm-nee-o)
nausea, el asco (ás-ko)
nurse, la enfermera (en-fer-máy-ra)
operation, la operación (o-pay-ra-thee-ón)
pain, el dolor (do-lór)
patient, el enfermo (en-fér-mo)
poison, el veneno (vay-náy-no)
policeman, el guardia (gwár-dee-a)
remedy, el remedio (ray-máy-dhee-o)
spot, la maca (má-ka)
sprain, la torcedura (tor-thay-dhōō-ra)
sting, la picadura (pee-ka-dhōō-ra)
stomach ache, el dolor de estómago (do-lór day es-tó-ma-go)
stye, el orzuelo (or-thoo-áy-lo)
sunstroke, la insolación (een-so-la-thee-ón)
surgeon, el cirujano (thee-roo-há-no)
surgery, el consultorio (kon-sool-tó-ree-o)
swelling, la tumefacción (too-may-fak-thee-ón)
temperature, la temperatura (taym-payr-a-tōō-ra)
toothache, el dolor de muelas (do-lór day moo-áy-las)
treatment, el tratamiento (tra-ta-mee-én-to)
wound, la herida (ay-rēē-dha)
X-ray, la radiografía (ra-dhee-o-gra-fēē-a)

There has been an accident.   Ha habido un accidente.
        a a-bēē-dho oon ak-thee-dhén-tay

Call a policeman quickly.   Llame rápido un guardia.
        lyá-may rá-pee-dho oon gwár-dee-a

Call an ambulance (the emergency service).
Haga mandar una ambulancia (el servicio de urgencia).
á-ga man-dár ōō-na am-boo-lán-thee-a (ser-vēē-thee-o day oor-hén-thee-a)

Is there a doctor near here?
¿Hay un médico cerca de aquí?
á-ee oon máy-dhee-ko thér-ka day a-kēē

Someone has fallen in the water.
Alguien ha caído al agua.
ál-gee-en a ka-ēē-dho al á-gwa

He (she) is seriously injured.
Está gravemente herido(a).
es-tá gra-vay-mén-tay ay-rēē-dho(a)

He (she) has been run over.
Ha sido atropellado(a).
a sēē-dho a-tro-payl-yá-dho(a)

He (she) is losing blood.
Pierde la sangre.
pee-áyr-day la sán-gray

He has lost consciousness.
Ha perdido el sentido.
a per-dēē-dho el sen-tēē-dho

He has fainted.
Se ha desmayado.
say a des-ma-yá-dho

He has burnt (cut) his face.
Se ha quemado (cortado) la cara.
say a kay-má-dho (kor-tá-dho) la ká-ra

It is bleeding.
Echa sangre.
áy-cha sán-gray

It is swollen.
Está entumecido.
es-tá en-too-may-thēē-dho

Who is responsible for the accident?
¿Quién ha causado el accidente?
kee-én a kow-sá-dho el ak-thee-dén-tay

Have you any bandages?
¿Tiene usted vendas?
tee-áy-nay oos-taydh vén-das

Can you dress this wound?
¿Puede usted curar esta herida?
poo-áy-dhay oos-táydh koo-rár és-ta ay-rēē-dha

Can you make a splint?
¿Sabe usted hacer una tablilla?
sá-bay oos-táydh a-thér ōō-na ta-blēēl-ya

Bring hot (cold) water (a blanket).

Traiga agua caliente (fría) (una manta).

trá-ee-ga á-gwa ka-lee-én-tay (frēē-a) (ōō-na mán-ta)

He (she) ought to be X-rayed.

Deberían hacerle una radiografía.

deb-ay-rēē-an a-thér-lay ōō-na ra-dhee-o-gra-fēē-a

Help me to carry him (her).

Ayúdeme a llevarle (la).

a-yōō-dhay-may a lyay-vár-le(la)

Don't move the injured.

No mueva al (a la) herido(a).

no moo-áy-va al (a la) ay-rēē-dho(a)

He (she) is not well.

No está bien.

no es-tá bee-én

I am feeling very ill. Please send for the doctor.

Me siento muy enfermo(a). Mande buscar al médico, por favor.

may see-én-to mwee en-fér-mo(a). mán-day boos-kár al máy-dhee-ko por fa-vór

I have a pain in ...

Me duele ...

may doo-áy-lay ..

Do you feel any pain here?

¿ Le duele aquí?

lay doo-áy-lay a-kēē

Show me your tongue.

Enséñeme la lengua.

en-sáyn-yay-may la lén-gwa

I am not sleeping well.

No duermo.

no doo-ér-mo

I cannot eat.

No puedo comer.

no poo-áy-dho ko-mér

I have no appetite.

No tengo apetito.

no tén-go a-pay-tēē-to

I have a stomach ache.

Tengo dolor de estómago.

tén-go do-lór day es-tó-ma-go

I feel giddy.

La cabeza se me vuelve.

la ka-báy-tha say may voo-áyl-vay

I think I have food poisoning.

Creo haber comido algo en malas condiciones.

kráy-o a-bér ko-mēē-dho ál-go en má-las kon-dee-thee-ó-nays

Will you give me a prescription? ¿Quiere usted darme una receta?

kee-áy-ray oos-táydh dár-may ōō-na ray-tháy-ta

What must I do? ¿Qué debo hacer?

kay dáy-bo a-thér

Should I stay in bed? ¿Guardo la cama?

gwár-do la ká-ma

I feel better. Me siento mejor.

may see-én-to may-hór

When will you come and see me again? ¿Cuándo volverá usted a verme?

kwán-do vol-vay-rá oos-táydh a vér-may

How much is your fee, doctor? ¿Cuánto es su honorario, doctor?

kwán-to es soo o-no-rá-ree-o, dok-tór

Where is there a chemist who will make up this prescription? ¿Dónde hay una farmacia que me haga esta receta?

dón-day á-ee ōō-na far-má-thee-a kay may á-ga és-ta ray-tháy-ta

Can you recommend a dentist? ¿Puede usted recomendarme un dentista?

poo-áy-dhay oos-táydh ray-ko-men-dhár-may oon den-tēēs-ta

Can you give me an appointment for Monday? ¿Puede usted darme cita para el lunes?

poo-áy-dhay oos-táydh dár-may thēē-ta pá-ra el lōō-nays

I have toothache. Tengo dolor de muelas.

tén-go do-lór day moo-áy-las

It aches a lot; I cannot wait. Duele mucho; no puedo esperar.

doo-áy-lay mōō-cho; no poo-áy-dho es-pay-rár

Will you extract it? ¿Quiere usted sacármelo?

kee-áy-ray oos-táydh sa-kár-may-lo

Can you save it? ¿Puede salvarlo?

poo-áy-dhay sal-vár-lo

I have lost a filling. He perdido una empastadura.

ay per-dēē-dho ōō-na em-pas-ta-dhōō-ra

I am going to fill it.	Voy a empastarlo.
	voy a em-pas-tár-lo
You are hurting me.	Me hace daño.
	may á-thay dán-yo
I prefer gas (an injection).	Prefiero el gas (una inyección).
	pray-fee-áy-ro el gas (ōō-na een-yek-thee-ón)
My gums are swollen (are bleeding).	Mis encías están hinchadas (echan sangre).
	mees en-thēē-as es-tán een-chá-dhas (áy-chan sán-gray)
I have broken my dentures.	He roto mi dentadura.
	ay ró-to mee den-ta-dhōō-ra
Can you repair it quickly?	¿Puede arreglarla rápido?
	poo-áy-dhay a-ray-glár-la rá-pee-dho

PLACES AND INHABITANTS

Africa, Africa, africano (á-free-ka, a-free-ká-no)
Andalusia, Andalucía, andaluz (an-da-loo-thēē-a, an-da-lúth)
Aragon, Aragón, aragonés (a-ra-gón, a-ra-go-nés)
Argentina, la Argentina, argentino (ar-hen-tēē-na, ar-hen-tēē-no)
Asturias, Asturias, asturiano (as-tōō-ree-as, as-too-ree-á-no)
Australia, Australia, australiano (ows-trá-lee-a, ows-tra-lee-á-no)
Austria, Austria, austríaco (óws-tree-a, ows-trēē-a-ko)
Basque provinces, Vascongadas, vasco, vascuence (vas-kon-gá-das, vás-ko, vas-kwén-thay)
Belgium, Bélgica, belga (bél-hee-ka, bél-ga)
Bolivia, Bolivia, boliviano (bo-lēē-vee-a, bo-lee-vee-á-no)
Brazil, el Brasil, brasileño (bra-sēēl, bra-see-láyn-yo)
Canada, el Canadá, canadiense (ka-na-dhá, ka-na-dhee-én-say)
Castile, Castilla, castillano (kas-tēēl-ya, kas-teel-yá-no)
Catalonia, Cataluña, catalán (ka-ta-lōōn-ya, ka-ta-lán)
Chile, Chile, chileno (chēē-lay, chee-láy-no)
Colombia, Colombia, colombiano (ko-lóm-bee-a, ko-lom-bee-á-no)
Ecuador, el Ecuador, ecuatoriano (ay-kwa-dhór, ay-kwa-to-ree-á-no)
England, Inglaterra, inglés (een-gla-táy-ra, een-gláys)
Extremadura, Extremadura, extremeño (ex-tray-ma-dhōō-ra, ex-tray-máyn-yo)
France, Francia, francés (frán-thee-a, fran-thés)
Galicia, Galicia, gallego (ga-lēē-thee-a, gal-yáy-go)
Germany, Alemania, alemán (a-lay-má-nee-a, a-lay-mán)
Great Britain, la Gran Bretaña, británico (gran bray-tán-ya, bree-tá-nee-ko)
Greece, Grecia, griego (gráy-thee-a, gree-áy-go)
India, la India, indio (ēēn-dee-a, ēēn-dee-o)
Ireland, Irlanda, irlandés (eer-lan-da, eer-lan-dés)

Israel, Israel, judío (ees-ra-él, hoo-dēē-o)
Italy, Italia, italiano (ee-tá-lee-a, ee-ta-lee-á-no)
Majorca, Mallorca, mallorquin (mal-yór-ka, mal-yor-kēēn)
Malaga, Málaga, malagueño (má-la-ga, ma-la-gáyn-yo)
Mexico, Méjico, mejicano (máy-hee-ko, may-hee-ká-no)
Morocco, Marruecos, marroquí (mar-wáy-kos, ma-ro-kēē)
Navarre, Navarra, navarrés (na-vá-ra, na-va-rés)
Netherlands, los Países Bajos, holandés (pa-ēē-says bá-hos, o-lan-dés)
New Zealand, la Nueva Zelanda, nuevazelandés (noo-áy-va thay-lán-da, noo-áy-va-thay-lan-dés)
Norway, Noruega, noruego (nor-wáy-ga, nor-wáy-go)
Panama, el Panamá, panameño (pa-na-má, pa-na-máyn-yo)
Paraguay, el Paraguay, paraguayo (pa-ra-goo-á-ee, pa-ra-goo-á-yo)
Peru, el Perú, peruviano (pay-rōō, pay-roo-vee-á-no)
Porto Rico, Puerto Rico, puertoriqueño (pwáyr-to rēē-ko, pwayr-to-ree-káyn-yo)
Portugal, Portugal, portugués, (por-too-gál, por-too-gáys)
Russia, la Unión Soviética, ruso (oo-nee-ón so-vee-áy-tee-ka, rōō-so)
Scotland, Escocia, escocés (es-kó-thee-a, es-ko-thés)
Seville, Sevilla, sevillano (say-vēēl-ya, say-veel-yá-no)
South America, la América del sur, suramericano (a-máy-ree-ka del soor, soor-a-may-ree-ká-no)
Spain, España, español (es-pán-ya, es-pan-yól)
Sweden, Suecia, sueco (swáy-thee-a, swáy-ko)
Switzerland, Suiza, suizo (swēē-tha, swēē-tho)
Tangiers, Tánger (tán-her)
Uruguay, el Uruguay, uruguayo (oo-roo-gwá-ee, oo-roo-gwá-yo)
U.S.A., los Estados Unidos, norteamericano (es-tá-dhos oo-nēē-dos, nor-tay-a-may-ree-ká-no)
Venezuela, Venezuela, venezolano (vay-nay-thoo-áy-la, vay-nay-tho-lá-no)
Wales, El País de Gales, galés (pa-ēēs day gá-lays, ga-láys)

STUDENT LIFE AND AU PAIR

VOCABULARY

bursary, la beca (báy-ka)
certificate, el diploma (dee-pló-ma)
class, la clase (klá-say)
course, el curso (kōōr-so)
examination, el examen (ex-á-men)
excellent, sobresaliente (so-bray-sa-lee-én-tay)
fee, la matrícula (ma-trēē-koo-la)
homesickness, la añoranza (an-yo-rán-tha)
housework, los quehaceres domésticos (kay-a-tháy-rays do-máys-tee-kos)
lecture, la conferencia (kon-fay-rén-thee-a)
lecturer, el(la) conferenciante (kon-fay-ren-thee-án-tay)

lodging, el alojamiento (a-lo-ha-mee-én-to)
note, to, apuntar (a-poon-tár)
notebook, el cuaderno (kwa-dáyr-no)
pocket money, el dinero para gastos pequeños (dee-náy-ro pá-ra gás-tos pay-káyn-yos)
professor, el catedrático (ka-tay-drá-tee-ko)
student, el(la) estudiante (es-too-dhee-án-tay)
term, el trimestre (tree-máys-tray)
thesis, la tesis (táy-sees)
tutor, el tutor (too-tór)
university, la universidad (oo-nee ver-see-dádh)

Welcome to . . . Sea el(la) bienvenido(a) a . . .
sáy-a el (la) bee-en-vay-nēē-dho (dha) a . . .

Did you have a good journey? ¿Ha hecho un buen viaje?
a áy-cho oon boo-én vee-á-hay

Do you need anything? ¿Le hace falta algo?
lay á-thay fál-ta ál-go

Is there anything you don't eat? ¿Hay algo que no come?
á-ee ál-go kay no kó-may

I can't eat . . . No puedo comer . . .
no poo-áy-dho ko-mér . . .

I shall give you . . . per week Le daré . . . por semana para
pocket-money. sus gastos pequeños.
lay da-ray . . . por say-má-na pá-ra soos gás-tos pay-káyn-yos

Will you help with the house- ¿Quiere usted ayudar con los
work (shopping, washing-up, quehaceres domésticos (a
to look after the children)? hacer las compras, a lavar la
vajilla, a cuidar a los niños)?
kee-áy-ray oos-táydh a-yoo-dhár kon los kay-a-thér-ays do-máys-tee-kos (a a-thér las kóm-pras, a la-vár la va-hēēl-ya, a kwee-dhár a los nēēn-yos)

Could you take the children to ¿Quiere usted llevar a los
school? niños a la escuela?
kee-áy-ray oos-táydh lyay-vár a los nēēn-yos a la es-kwáy-la

May I go out? ¿Puedo salir?
pwáy-dho sa-lēēr

Where is the Catholic (Protestant) church?
¿Dónde está la iglesia católica (protestante)?
dón-day es-tá la ee-gláy-see-a ka-tó-lee-ka (pro-tays-tán-tay)

At what time is mass?
¿A qúe hora se dice la misa?
a kay ó-ra say dēē-thay la mēē-sa

I want to go to confession.
Quiero confesarme.
kee-áy-ro kon-fay-sár-may

Have you written to your parents?
¿Ha escrito a sus padres?
a es-krēē-to a soos pá-drays

Where is the faculty of arts (law, science, medicine)?
¿Dónde está la facultad d letras (derecho, ciencias medicina)?
dón-day es-tá la fa-kool-tádh day láy-tras (day-ráy-cho, thee-én-thee-as, may-dhay thēē-na)

Where can I enrol for . . . ?
¿Dónde puedo matricularm para . . . ?
dón-day poo-áy-dho ma-tree-koo-lár-may pá-ra . . .

Are there any courses for foreigners?
¿Hay cursos para extranjeros
á-ee kōōr-sos pá-ra ex-tran-háy-ros

Does one get a certificate?
¿Se otorga un diploma?
say o-tór-ga oon dee-pló-ma

A course not leading to a certificate or degree.
Un curso sin efectos acadé micos.
oon kōōr-so seen ay-fék-tos a-ka-dháy-mee-kos

Where can I pay the fee?
¿Dónde puedo pagar la ma trícula?
dón-day poo-áy-dho pa-gár la ma-trēē-koo-la

I am looking for lodgings.
Busco alojamiento.
bōōs-ko a-lo-ha-mee-én-to

Where is the library (reading room)?
¿Dónde está la biblioteca (sala de lectura)?
dón-day es-tá la bee-blee-o-táy-ka (sá-la day lek-tōō-ra)

Is there a students' club (restaurant)?

¿Hay un club (restaurante) para estudiantes?

á-ee oon kloob (res-tow-rán-tay) pá-ra es-too-dhee-án-tays

Is there a reduction in price for students?

¿Hay una rebaja para los estudiantes?

á-ee ōō-na ray-bá-ha pá-ra los es-too-dhee-án-tays

Here is my student's card.

Aquí tiene usted mi tarjeta de estudiante.

a-kēē tee-áy-nay oos-táydh mee tar-háy-ta day es-too-dhee-án-tay

MONEY

Banks are open from about 9 a.m. to 1 p.m. and for a time in the afternoon. Like shops they have a longer break in the middle of the day from May to October. Only the cashier pays out money and this only on surrender of a numbered ticket obtained from the window where one has done business. A quarter of an hour often elapses between obtaining a ticket and the cashier calling one's number. When cashing a traveller's cheque one is required to show one's passport and give an address. There is a charge (not everywhere the same) of a few pesetas for cashing a cheque and stamp duty of a few cents.

VOCABULARY

bank, el banco (bán-ko)
cashier's window, pagos (pá-gos)
cheque, el cheque (cháy-kay)
dollars, dólares (dó-la-rays)
exchange, el cambio (kám-bee-o)
francs, francos (frán-kos)
letter of credit, la carta de crédito (kár-ta day kráy-dhee-to)
note, el billete (beel-yáy-tay)
pound sterling, la libra esterlina (lēē-bra es-ter-lēē-na)
rate of exchange, el cambio (kám-bee-o)
traveller's cheque, el cheque de viajero (cháy-kay day vee-a-háy-ro)
window, la ventanilla (vayn-ta-nēēl-ya)

Is there a bank near here?

¿Hay un banco cerca de aquí?

á-ee oon bán-ko tháyr-ka day a-kēē

| At what time does the bank open? | ¿A qué hora se abre el banco? |

a kay ó-ra say á-bray el bán-ko

| I should like to cash a cheque. | Deseo cambiar un cheque. |

day-sáy-o kam-bee-ár oon cháy-kay

| What is the pound at? | ¿A cuánto está la libra? |

a kwán-to es-tá la lēē-bra

| Sign here please. | Firme aquí por favor. |

fēēr-may a-kēē por fa-vór

| How would you like it? | ¿Cómo lo quiere usted? |

kó-mo lo kee-áy-ray oos-táydh

| One large note and the rest small. | Un billete grande y los demás pequeños. |

oon beel-yáy-tay grán-day ee los day-más pay-káyn-yos

TABLES

The following units of currency are used. The traveller should work out for himself or herself a few useful equivalents at the prevailing rate and note them in the space provided.

SPAIN

100 céntimos (tháyn-tee-mos)=1 peseta (pay-sáy-ta)

| £1 | = | 50p | = | 25p | = | 5p | = |
| 5 dollars | = | 2 dollars | = | 1 dollar | = | 50 cents | = |

ARGENTINA, MEXICO

100 centavos (thayn-tá-vos)=1 peso (páy-so)

| £1 | = | 50p | = | 25p | = | 5p | = |
| 5 dollars | = | 2 dollars | = | 1 dollar | = | 50 cents | = |

NUMBERS

1 =uno (ōō-no) [un, una (oon, ōō-na) before a noun]
2 =dos (dos)
3 =tres (trays)
4 =cuatro (kwá-tro)
5 =cinco (thēēn-ko)
6 =seis (sáy-ees)
7 =siete (see-áy-tay)
8 =ocho (ó-cho)
9 =nueve (noo-áy-vay)
10 =diez (dee-áyth)
11 =once (ón-thay)
12 =doce (dó-thay)
13 =trece (tráy-thay)
14 =catorce (ka-tór-thay)
15 =quince (kēēn-thay)
16 =dieciseis (dee-ayth-ee-sáy-ees)
17 =diecisiete (dee-ayth-ee-see-áy-tay)
18 =dieciocho (dee-ayth-ee-ó-cho)
19 =diecinueve (dee-ayth-ee-noo-áy-vay)
20 =veinte (váy-een-tay)
21 =veintiuno (*see* uno) (vay-een-tee-ōō-no)
22 =veintidos (vay-een-tee-dhós)
30 =treinta (tráy-een-ta)
31 =treinta y uno (tray-een-ta ee ōō-no)
32 =treinta y dos (tray-een-ta ee dós)
40 =cuarenta (kwa-rén-ta)
41 =cuarenta y uno (kwa-rén-ta ee ōō-no)
50 =cincuenta (theen-kwáyn-ta)
51 =cincuenta y uno (thee-kwáyn-ta ee ōō-no)
60 =sesenta (say-sáyn-ta)
61 =sesenta y uno (say-sáyn-ta ee ōō-no)
70 =setenta (say-tén-ta)
71 =setenta y uno (say-ten-ta ee ōō-no)
80 =ochenta (o-cháyn-ta)
81 =ochenta y uno (o-cháyn-ta ee ōō-no)
90 =noventa (no-váyn-ta)
91 =noventa y uno (no-váyn-ta ee ōō-no)
100 =ciento (thee-áyn-to) [cien (thee-áyn) before a noun]
200 =doscientos(as) (dos-thee-áyn-tos/as)
300 =trescientos(as) (trays-thee-áyn-tos/as)
1,000 =mil (meel)
2,000 =dos mil (dos meel)
1 million =un millón (oon meel-yón)

1st =primero (pree-máy-ro)
2nd =segundo (say-gōōn-do)
3rd =tercero (tayr-tháy-ro)
4th =cuarto (kwár-to)
5th =quinto (kēēn-to)
6th =sexto (sáys-to)
7th =septimo (sáy-tee-mo)
8th =octavo (ok-tá-vo)
9th =noveno (no-váy-no)
10th =décimo (dáy-thee-mo)

From here on one uses the cardinal numbers *uno*, *dos*, etc., with the exceptions of *vigésimo* (vee-háy-see-mo), 20th; and *centésimo* (thayn-táy-see-mo) 100th.

half, la mitad (mee-tádh), but ½ **kilo** =medio kilo (máy-dhee-o
half asleep, medio dormido (máy-dhee-o dor-mēē-do)
a quarter, un cuarto (kwár-to)
a third, un tercio (táyr-thee-o)
two thirds, los dos tercios (dos táyr-thee-os)
a fifth, la quinta parte (kēēn-ta pár-tay)

CONVERSION TABLES

DISTANCE

Kilómetros		Miles	Miles		Kilómetros
1	approx.	$\frac{5}{8}$	1	approx.	1·6
2	,,	$1\frac{1}{4}$	2	,,	3·2
3	,,	$1\frac{7}{8}$	3	,,	4·8
4	,,	$2\frac{1}{2}$	4	,,	6·4
5	,,	$3\frac{1}{8}$	5	,,	8
6	,,	$3\frac{3}{4}$	6	,,	9·6
7	,,	$4\frac{3}{8}$	7	,,	11·3
8	,,	5	8	,,	12·9
9	,,	$5\frac{5}{8}$	9	,,	14·5
10	,,	$6\frac{1}{4}$	10	,,	16·1
15	,,	$9\frac{3}{8}$	15	,,	24·1
20	,,	$12\frac{1}{2}$	20	,,	32·2
25	,,	$15\frac{5}{8}$	25	,,	40·2
30	,,	$18\frac{3}{4}$	30	,,	48·3
35	,,	$21\frac{7}{8}$	35	,,	56·3
40	,,	25	40	,,	64·4
45	,,	$28\frac{1}{8}$	45	,,	72·4
50	,,	$31\frac{1}{8}$	50	,,	80·5
55	,,	$34\frac{3}{8}$	55	,,	88·5
60	,,	$37\frac{1}{2}$	60	,,	96·6
65	,,	$40\frac{5}{8}$	65	,,	104·6
70	,,	$43\frac{3}{4}$	70	,,	112·7
75	,,	$46\frac{7}{8}$	75	,,	120·7
80	,,	50	80	,,	128·7
85	,,	$53\frac{1}{8}$	85	,,	136·8
90	,,	$56\frac{1}{4}$	90	,,	144·8
95	,,	$59\frac{3}{8}$	95	,,	152·9
100	,,	$62\frac{1}{2}$	100	,,	161

N.B. A rough way to convert kilometres to miles: divide the kilometres by 8 and multiply by 5. E.g. 32 kms. ÷8 =4 ×5 =20 miles.
Vice versa, to convert miles to kilometres divide by 5 and multiply by 8. E.g. 35 miles ÷5 =7 ×8 =56 kms.

LENGTH

Centímetros		Feet	Inches	Feet	Inches		Centímetros
1	approx.		2/5″		1″	approx.	2·5
5	,,		2″		3″	,,	7·5
10	,,		4″		6″	,,	15
15	,,		6″		9″	,,	22·5
20	,,		8″	1′		,,	30·5
25	,,		10″	1′	6″	,,	45·5
50	,,	1′	8″	2′		,,	61
75	,,	2′	6″	2′	6″	,,	75
100 (1 metro)		3′	3″	3′		,,	91·5

ALTITUDE

Metros		Feet	Feet		Metros
25	approx.	82	50	approx.	15
50	,,	164	75	,,	23
75	,,	246	100	,,	31
100	,,	328	250	,,	76
250	,,	820	500	,,	152
500	,,	1,640	1,000	,,	305
1,000	,,	3,281	2,000	,,	610
2,000	,,	6,562	3,000	,,	915
3,000	,,	9,843	4,000	,,	1,220
4,000	,,	13,124	5,000	,,	1,525

N.B. To convert metres roughly to yards multiply by 12 and divide by 11.
E.g. 100 metres × 12 = 1,200 ÷ 11 = 109 yards.

LIQUID MEASURES

Litros		Pints and Gallons		Gallons			Litros
1	approx.	1¾ pints		⅛ (1 pint)	approx.		0·57
2	,,	3½	,,	¼ (2 pints)	,,		1·15
3	,,	5¼	,,	½ (4 pints)	,,		2·3
4	,,	7	,,	¾ (6 pints)	,,		3·42
5	,,	1·1 gallons		1	,,		4·5
6	,,	1·3	,,	2	,,		9·1
7	,,	1·5	,,	3	,,		13·6
8	,,	1·8	,,	4	,,		18·2
9	,,	2·0	,,	5	,,		22·7

Litros		Pints and Gallons		Gallons			Litros
10	approx.	2·2 gallons		6	approx.		27·3
20	,,	4·4	,,	7		,,	31·8
30	,,	6·6	,,	8		,,	36·4
40	,,	8·8	,,	9		,,	40·9
50	,,	11·0	,,	10		,,	45·5

WEIGHTS AND MEASURES

VOCABULARY

depth, la profundidad (pro-foon-dee-dhádh)
height, la altura (al-tōō-ra)
length, la longitud (lon-hee-tōōdh)
measure, la medida (may-dhēē-dha)
thickness, la espesura (es-pay-sōō-ra)
weight, el peso (páy-so)
width (breadth), la anchura (an-chōō-ra)

What is the weight of?
¿ Cuánto pesa . . . ?
kwán-to páy-sa . .

What is the depth (height, length, thickness, width) of . . . ?
¿ Cuánto tiene de profundo (alto, largo, espeso, ancho) . . . ?
kwán-to tee-áyn-ay day pro-fōōn-do (ál-to, lár-go, es-páy-so, án-cho) . . .

It is five metres long by ten metres wide.
Tiene cinco metros de largo por diez metros de ancho.
tee-áy-nay thēēn-ko máy-tros day lár-go por dee-áyth máy-tros day án-cho

CONVERSION TABLES

WEIGHTS

Gramos		Ounces	Ounces		Gramos
50	approx.	1¾	1	approx.	28
100	,,	3½	2	,,	56
125	,,	4¼	5	,,	142
250	,,	8¾	8 (½ lb.)	,,	227
500	,, 1 lb.	1½	12	,,	340
1,000 (1 kilo)	,, 2 lbs.	3	16 (1 lb.)	,,	453

Kilos		Pounds	Stones			Kilos
5	approx.	11	1 (14 lb.)	approx.		6·35
10	,,	22	7 (98 ,,)	,,		44·5
15	,,	33	8 (112 ,,)	,,		51
20	,,	44	9 (126 ,,)	,,		57
25	,,	55	10 (140 ,,)	,,		63·5
30	,,	66	11 (154 ,,)	,,		70
40	,,	88	12 (168 ,,)	,,		76
50	,,	110	13 (182 ,,)	,,		82·5
75	,,	165	14 (196 ..)	,,		89
100	,,	220	15 (210 ,,)	,,		95

PRESSURE (TYRES)

Lb. per sq. in.		Kg. per sq. cm.	Kg. per sq. cm.		Lb. per sq. in.
16	approx.	1·12	1·1	approx.	16·0
18	,,	1·27	1·3	,,	18·5
20	,,	1·41	1·4	,,	19·9
22	,,	1·55	1·6	,,	22·8
24	,,	1·69	1·7	,,	24·2
26	,,	1·83	1·8	,,	25·6
28	,,	1·97	2·0	,,	28·4
30	,,	2·11	2·1	,,	29·9

TEMPERATURE

Fahrenheit °F	Centigrade °C	Fahrenheit °F	Centigrade °C
212 (Boiling)	100	59	15
104	40	50	10
102	38·9	41	5
101	38·3	32 (Freezing)	0
100	37·8	28	−2
98·4 (Body)	37	23	−5
97	36·1	18	−8
86	30	12	−11
80	26·7	5	−15
77	25	0	−18
68	20	−4	−20
64	17·8		

CLOTHING SIZES

DRESSES AND SUITS (Women)

British	36	38	40	42	44	46
American	34	36	38	40	42	44
Continental	42	44	46	48	50	52

DRESSES AND SUITS (Junior Miss)

British	32	33	35	36	38	39
American	10	12	14	16	18	20
Continental	38	40	42	44	46	48

MEN'S SUITS AND OVERCOATS

British and American	36	38	40	42	44	46
Continental	46	48	50	52	54	56

SHIRTS

British and American	14	$14\frac{1}{2}$	15	$15\frac{1}{2}$	16	$16\frac{1}{2}$	17
Continental	36	37	38	39	41	42	43

SOCKS

British and American	$9\frac{1}{2}$	10	$10\frac{1}{2}$	11	$11\frac{1}{2}$
Continental	38-39	39-40	40-41	41-42	42-43

HATS

British and American	$6\frac{1}{2}$	$6\frac{5}{8}$	$6\frac{3}{4}$	$6\frac{7}{8}$	7	$7\frac{1}{8}$	$7\frac{1}{4}$	$7\frac{3}{8}$	$7\frac{1}{2}$
Continental	53	54	55	56	57	58	59	60	61

SHOES

British and American	3	4	5	6	7	8	9	10
Continental	36	37	38	39	41	42	43	44

STOCKINGS

British and American	8	$8\frac{1}{2}$	9	$9\frac{1}{2}$	10	$10\frac{1}{2}$
Continental	0	1	2	3	4	5

GLOVE sizes are the same in every country.

VOCABULARIO

INDEX